TEACHER'S MANUAL

to accompany

WE, THE ALIEN

AN INTRODUCTION TO CULTURAL ANTHROPOLOGY

Paul Bohannan

Test Bank prepared by

Robbie Davis-Floyd

WAVELAND
PRESS, INC.

Prospect Heights, Illinois

For information about this book, write or call:

Waveland Press, Inc.
P.O. Box 400
Prospect Heights, Illinois 60070
(708) 634-0081

Contents

Introduction   1

  1 Anthropology, Culture and Society   5

  2 Learning Culture   13

  3 Men and Women, Sex and Babies   19

  4 Marriage and Family   27

  5 Kinship and Community   35

  6 Bread and Work   45

  7 Conflict and Order   53

  8 Getting Control   63

  9 Born Equal?   73

 10 Symbols: Language and Art   87

 11 Meaning: Creativity and Performance   97

 12 Creed: Religion and Ideology   107

 13 How Culture Works   121

 14 From Colonialism to Global Society   131

 15 Anthropology in a Global Society   143

Appendixes   157

The aims of the Teacher's Manual are simple: (1) to explain the prominence given to premises and propositions at the beginning of each chapter, and to say something about the workbook of projects and other activities in *Discovering The Alien*, which has been designed to accompany the textbook, (2) to provide a short, annotated list of films that can profitably be used with *We, The Alien*, with information about current availability, and (3) to provide a large bank of test questions from which instructors can choose.

Propositions and Premises

Each chapter of *We, The Alien* opens with a series of propositions and premises. Every anthropologist (indeed, every person) has premises that underlie his or her thinking in the same way that axioms underlie Euclidean geometry. Such premises form the basis for logical operations as well as for convictions and personal worldview.

Many of our premises are unconscious—they are either part of the culture that we have learned throughout life and never questioned, or else they result from our customary reactions to our personal experiences. Making unconscious premises overt is one of the major goals of cultural anthropology.

My goal has been to make my own premises that underlie this book as overt and as available as possible. The statements of "Propositions and Premises" that I have written for the text try to achieve clarity. The premises can then be judged—and so can the message of the book. Another goal is to get students to examine their own premises—and realize that their premises are not part of nature, but rather are cultural and/or personal axioms that underlie their thought.

If your students disagree with some of my premises, please remind them that, to refute the premises, it must be done on the basis either of data or of reason. They have to:

- find the data that proves the text's or the teacher's statement erroneous, and/or
- examine their own logical processes, and/or

- find their hidden premises that lead them logically, with accepted data, to the conclusions they have reached.

Then, students may be asked to formulate their own premises. Here again, they must do it on the basis of data and reason. Premises—and therefore any book (or any student paper) based on them—contain a statement of a worldview. If you or your students work out new and different premises, please let us hear from you.

Discovering The Alien

All student exercises have been put into a workbook, *Discovering The Alien*. There are far more projects—contributed by many anthropologists—in this workbook than a single semester provides time to do. Again, the goal is to provide as rich a resource as possible from which teachers can make choices.

Discovering The Alien also includes vocabulary exercises (not just technical terms), information on how to find a topic for a paper, and down-to-earth guides of how to write any of several kinds of academic papers.

The workbook also contains Cultures of the Imagination, which are akin to science fiction. I am serious about good science fiction. Cultures of the imagination provide an excellent means of anthropological simulation. They show up human characteristics, both cultural and non-cultural, as nothing else can. I have found that they also drive students to anthropological conclusions. Cultures of the imagination help us to play out assumptions or policies without going through the political difficulty and social agony of having to try them out. These imaginary ethnographies have the advantage that students can examine specific points, then follow them out from one part of the culture to another. They prove, over and over, that all parts of cultures are connected.

Finally, the workbook contains a section of puzzles for each chapter—double crostics, word-search puzzles, and several other forms of puzzles.

Feedback

We want as much feedback as you are willing to give us on the whole project. What else should be included in the Teacher's Manual? What else should be in future editions of the workbook? If you have successful projects, send them to us. If we publish them, you will be given full credit. Do puzzles work as teaching tools? Do some work better than others?

What about the text did students particularly like? What did they dislike? Were there parts they had trouble reading? What would they like to know more about? Either Paul Bohannan or the Waveland editors will acknowledge all communications—please let us know what needs renewing and what works already.

Special Terms

I have made every effort to avoid specialized terminology in this book. The only place I feel I have not solved this problem is in the chapters on kinship. It is almost impossible to talk about kinship without a whole barrage of terms.

I do, however, use one highly-specialized term throughout the book. Some anthropologists will object to the verb *culturize* which I introduce in the first chapter, then use throughout the book. Explanation is in order.

The word *culture* is a noun. Using it as a noun leads us to analyze it into parts, which are also nouns, and to examine the way the parts fit together. Fine. But our using it as a noun makes us think that it needs a verb. When culture is a noun, somebody must do something to it or with it.

Many years ago, Leslie White used the word culture as a verb: to culture, culturing. That turns culture into a predicate. Culturing occurs—and it happens to something else. It isn't a thing that is acted on, it is the action. White's usage never caught on—for good reason: our theories of cultural processes do not require that kind of general verb. Today one can read many demands that anthropologists turn to the study of *process* in order to supplement our ideas of structure—even to replace them. However, few explanations have been offered of just what studying process involves. The theory of cultural processes (although it has concerned a few anthropologists from time to time at least since van Gennep) has remained inadequately worked out. At least part of the difficulty is our seeing culture as a noun.

The verb *culturize* takes a different tack: it means that something has been subjected to a special kind of process. Although that verb can probably be used of other things, my primary interest is two-fold.

First, human beings behave as animals just as much as any other animals. However, all human animal behavior is culturized: it is thought about, discussed, and evaluated abstractly. Human beings do not merely behave, but they know they behave, and they talk about correct and incorrect behavior. When we compare human behavior with that of other primates or other animals, we must always keep in mind that there is a special dimension to human behavior—the cultural dimension—that is lacking in the behavior of other species. Because the cultural dimension affects all human behavior at all times, it can never be forgotten. To compare human behavior—any human behavior—to that of other animals without taking culture into account is instantly to falsify the human behavior. Culturization processes have changed everything, while leaving the life processes intact, just as the life processes have changed everything while leaving the chemical processes intact.

Second, human beings share several modes of social organization with other animals. However, human social organization is always culturized. For example, hierarchy among all primates is a matter of acknowledged individual strength and capacity. Among human beings it may be that, but is always more: cultural principles including justification and justice are added. Human beings do not merely associate with those present (or else change groups, which many animals do) but they also culturize their relationships and groups, giving them names and tasks and principles and doctrines and ideologies. Human social behavior cannot occur unless our animal behavior is culturized.

Thus, for immediate purposes, I am assuming that although chimpanzees and perhaps some other primates have been shown to use rudimentary culture, and although many species of animals—certainly all mammals—must learn a great deal, nevertheless the human investment in culture means we can presume that only human behavior and human society is thoroughly culturized.

Dogs and horses can learn some human culture. Their interaction with human beings may be to that small degree culturized. This is a quibble, but I have found that students raise the issue about their pets, so we have to be prepared to deal with it.

Illustrations

In the course of this textbook, all photographs, illustrations, tables, figures and a few statements in special type have been numbered serially. **The numbered captions provide a review of the main points in the chapter.** We consider this to be a valuable review tool for the student.

We have foregone a two-color or four-color process in this book on the assumption that the additional color adds considerable cost to the book without an equivalent addition to meaning or comprehension.

Words, Buzzwords and Glossary

Anthropology, like any other discipline, uses a lot of words that are not common in other contexts. That fact doesn't lead to any great difficulty. Far more difficult is the fact that they sometimes give special meanings to ordinary English words—such words may be difficult because the readers figure they already know what the word means.

In *We, The Alien*, a list of what we call buzzwords has been appended to the end of each chapter. Most of them are technical terms or words to which anthropologists give special meaning. Naturally, a glossary, which contains all of the buzzwords from the fifteen chapters as well as some other words, appears at the end of the book.

My personal conviction is that every student should have at his or her regular study place, and constantly be reminded to use, a good dictionary. Therefore, words that are readily found in the dictionary might not be found in the glossary *unless* anthropology has assigned special meanings for the word. Obviously, such a margin is a permeable one. For example, vodou went into the glossary. So did shaman. But invocation and sect did not—they are perfectly adequately defined in the dictionary.

In the workbook, *Discovering The Alien*, there is a list of fifty or more words for each chapter. Many ordinary English words are to be found there. We have not created special exercises for those vocabulary items, but merely listed them. Students who work with the lists will find their feel for words improved and their vocabularies enlarged.

The Bank of Test Questions

Our intention has been to provide as many test questions as is feasible—in many chapters, far more than can be used on any single quiz or exam. Again, the aim is to provide a rich resource for creating tests, not a finished product to be administered by rote.

We would appreciate your comments on how the test bank can be improved, just as we would appreciate them on how any other part of this exercise can be improved.

Films

For those instructors who wish to incorporate films into their courses, we have compiled an annotated starter list, by chapter (except Chapter 5), of films and videos currently available which have proven useful in the classroom and which will correspond nicely to the content of the specific chapter in *We, The Alien*. Depending upon your own experiences, other films, including fiction films, will be substituted. (See Appendix for up-to-date names, addresses, and telephone numbers of distributors cited in individual entries.)

The way that some aspects of cultural anthropology are well covered on film while others are not covered at all probably says something about the degree to which different aspects of culture can be conveyed visually. The same is true of illustrations in a book: some dimensions of culture are instantly clarified with visuals. Others would seem not to lend themselves to visualization at all. One of the subjects that visual anthropologists might get into is the limitations of visuals. To put it another way, in some contexts a picture may be worth a thousand words; but in other contexts, only a fool would try to use a picture if the right thousand words are available. This difficulty results in part from the fact that most theoretical statements are abstract. However, the topic is more complicated than that.

3

Anthropology, Culture and Society

1

What students should get out of the chapter . . .

Culture is a natural part of the world, just as matter and life are parts of the natural world. As life adds new dimensions and characteristics to matter, so culture adds new dimensions to life. Students should learn what culture is and some of the ways it affects individual and social life.

Cultural anthropology is, its practitioners insist, a "science," but we must not get hung up on that word. If we insist on this science point, biology is a better model than is physics for all social science, especially cultural anthropology.

The genius of cultural anthropology is that it achieves binocular vision about the human condition by taking two points of view: the point of view of the people who are being studied, and that of its environing culture (which includes the ideas and insights of anthropology).

Films and Videos

Baboon Behavior. 31 min. color. 1961. University of California Extension Media Center. Filmed in Kenya, this award-winning piece shows the many facets of baboon behavior that can be observed only in a natural environment. Explores the troop (the highly-integrated social unit of wild baboons) and emphasizes factors that foster social cohesion between the various ages and sexes composing it. Shows role of adult males in predator defense, attraction of the newborn infant, social aspect of grooming, and use of social gestures in maintaining troop organization. Traces infant behavior from close association with the mother at birth, through play in a group of juvenile peers, to the emergence of adult behavior patterns. Shows baboons together with many other species of animals, and makes frequent comparisons between pertinent aspects of baboon behavior and their counterparts in human development and behavior.

Franz Boas: 1852-1942. 59 min. color. Study guide available. Documentary Educational Resources. Uses reflections and anecdotes by scholars and students, archival photographs and film footage, and excerpts of his writings to present an in-depth profile of the German physicist who was responsible for shaping the methods of American anthropology. Interweaves the story of Boas' life and work with the story of the Kwakiutl Native Americans of the Northwest Coast, the principal subjects of Boas' fieldwork.

Ghurka Country. 19 min. color. 1967. University of California Extension Media Center. Cultural anthropologist John Hitchcock narrates this record of his study of the village of Musuri, Nepal, high in the Himalayas. The purpose of the study was to investigate the way people change their living habits in order to adapt to a mountain environment. Compares the relative abundance of lowland village life to harder life in the mountains, where people are very poor and cannot afford more than the food needed to stay alive. Shows a fishing party (their only group recreation), a magic dance to drive illness from a man into a chicken, a marriage party, and a religious ceremony in which chickens are sacrificed.

A Man Called Bee: Studying the Yanomamö. 42 min. color. 1974. Documentary Educational Resources. Shows anthropologist Napoleon Chagnon collecting field data, and explores some of the problems he faced in his work with the Yanomamö Indians of southern Venezuela. Includes considerable information about the Yanomamö, such as their system of kinship ties, their religious beliefs and ceremonies, and the growth and fissioning of their widely-scattered villages. Directed and narrated by Chagnon, this film provides viewers with a glimpse of themselves many generations removed in the past.

Margaret Mead's New Guinea Journal. 90 min. color. 1969. Indiana University Audio-Visual Center. Follows anthropologist Margaret Mead during her 1967 visit to the village of Peri, on Manus Island in New Guinea. She describes changes that have occurred since her visits in 1928 and 1953, as Peri leaped from the Stone Age to the twentieth century. Shows her discussing the problem of rebellious youth with village elders, whose views have changed since they were young.

Chapter 1

Test Items

True/False

1. Anthropology means the study of human beings.   T

2. A monocult is a person who speaks only one language.   F

3. Before writing an ethnography about another culture, the fieldworker should learn as much about his or her own culture as possible.   T

4. Anthropological fieldwork can be simultaneously an exciting and deeply threatening experience.   T

5. The most important rule in anthropological fieldwork is to make sure that the people you study understand what is important to you.   F

6. Biological anthropologists study the behavior of nonhuman primates.   T

7. Tools and meaning are two important characteristics of the human animal.   T

8. The four subfields of anthropology include biological anthropology, cultural anthropology, archaeology, and linguistics.   T

9. Language is important to cultural anthropologists because grammar and phonetics provide a model for organizing other aspects of culture.   T

10. A symbol *is* the thing it stands for.   F

11. Archaeologists study the material remains of past cultures.   T

12. Archaeology deals only with historical cultures, while cultural anthropology deals only with contemporary cultures.   F

13. Practicing anthropology and applied anthropology are widely divergent fields.   F

14. While practicing anthropology seeks to solve current problems, visionary anthropology asks how culture can be purposefully changed to improve the quality of life and the environment.   T

15. The major problem in transferring the ideas of visionary anthropology into the arena of practicing anthropology is popular acceptance of those ideas.   T

16. According to Bohannan, culture is what makes human animals human.   T

17. Culture is genetically transmitted.   F

18. All things are feedback systems.   F

19. Culture is a means for recording and sharing the results of successful and unsuccessful choices made by others.   T

20. Every human activity is culturized.   T

21. Society refers to the structure of relationships between groups, and between individuals as members of groups.   T

22. The principle of dominance allows primate relationships, once established, to proceed peacefully.   T

23. Experiences imposed by the environment as an individual grows up leaves a biological residue.   T

24. Long-term survival for the human species can be insured solely through the passing on of genes to the next generation.   F

25. Animals do not enter into social relationships.   F

26. Principles of social relationships shared by humans and animals include dominance, roles, ranking, and the specialization of tasks.   F

27. Principles of social relationships unique to humans include the cost-benefit principle and the principles of networking and the specialization of tasks.   F

28. Society is a survival mechanism.   T

29. The dyad is the basic social unit, and every stable dyad has its own culture.   T

30. Triads, categories, and groups are interchangeable concepts useful for the study of human social organization.   F

Multiple Choice

1. Biological anthropologists:
   a. are also known as physical anthropologists
   b. often study the behavior of nonhuman primates
   c. sometimes study human genetics
   d. seek to understand primate and human evolution
   * e. all of the above

2. Archaeologists:
   a. are restricted to studying only half of a culture
   b. use many of the natural sciences such as geology, biology, and hydrology to recreate as nearly as possible the lives and environments of earlier peoples
   c. do not use written records
   d. do not study the material culture of contemporary peoples
   * e. _____ and _____ (a and b)

3. Practicing anthropologists:
   a. are also known as applied anthropologists
   b. work in industry, government, and international agencies
   c. distinguish themselves from academic anthropologists
   d. work with immediate problems that need immediate answers
   e. none of the above
   * f. all of the above

4. Visionary anthropologists:
   a. seek to design innovative culture
   b. examine existing culture in search of new forms
   c. must make some culture invisible to mask its effects
   d. are concerned with the implications of long-term change
   * e. all of the above, except _____ (c)

5. Culture is:
    a. easily divisible into its parts
    b. genetically transmitted
    c. that which allows the creature to extend its capacities
    d. rare in the nonhuman world
 * e. ____ and ____ (c and d)
    f. all of the above

6. Some biological human behaviors shaped by culture include:
    a. eating, and defining what is edible and what is not
    b. elimination
    c. sexuality
    d. reproduction
    e. ____ and ____
 * f. all of the above

7. Basic principles shared by humans and apes include:
    a. the Principle of Dominance
    b. the Principle of Kinship
    c. the Principle of Role
    d. the Principle of Cooperation
    e. all of the above.
 * f. all of the above except ____ (c)

8. Principles unique to human social relationships include:
    a. the Principle of Contract
    b. the Principle of Specialization of Tasks
    c. the Principle of Ranking
    d. the Cost-Benefit Principle
    e. all of the above
 * f. all of the above except ____ (b)

9. Society:
    a. is a survival mechanism
    b. increases animals' capacity to carry out necessary tasks
    c. involves one animal's making changes in its behavior in response to other animals
    d. is a structure of relationships between individuals and groups
 * e. all of the above
    f. all of the above except ____

10. Dyads, triads, categories, groups, and networks:
    a. are rare in the human and primate worlds
    b. are all basic to primate survival
 * c. are useful anthropological distinctions between types of human social relationships
    d. all of the above

9

11. A network is:
    a. the same as a group
    b. a number of interlinked dyads
    c. sometimes the only principle that keeps people connected to one another in modern societies
    d. a fundamental principle of social relationship
  * e. all of the above except _____ (a)
    f. all of the above

12. A category is:
  * a. a cultural device for lumping people together
    b. the same as a group
    c. something given in nature and expressed in culture
    d. based on dyads
    e. all of the above except _____
    f. none of the above

Essay

1. What is an ethnography and what is its purpose?

2. Why does Bohannan say that translating a foreign language into English is a treacherous task?

3. What is the point of the story about the Tiv individual who allowed a man to drown and later became outraged to learn that Bohannan had not seen his mother for five years? How do you feel about it?

4. What does Bohannan mean when he says that knowing only one culture is a prison and that "we are ourselves the alien"?

5. What is the "anthropological attitude"? Evaluate the usefulness of this attitude in today's world.

6. List and describe the four basic fields of anthropology.

7. What is the difference between practicing and visionary anthropology? Why does Bohannan distinguish between them?

8. Define culture and discuss some of its primary characteristics.

9. What does Bohannan mean when he says that all human behavior carries a cultural overload?

10. Can you be a person without culture? Can you carry out relationships with other humans without culture? Why or why not?

11. Compare the roles of heritage, fate, and free choice in primate and human survival.

12. What is a symbol and what is the nature of its relationship to that which it symbolizes?

13. According to Bohannan, where is culture located, and what forms does it take?

14. Discuss the relationships between culture, learning, meaning, and behavior.

15. Briefly explain the concept of the selfish gene.

16. Name and discuss at least three of the principles of social relationships that Bohannan identifies as unique to humans, and explain how they differ from at least three of the principles of social relationships that humans and primates share.

17. Explain the distinctions between dyads, triads, categories, groups and networks and discuss the significance of these concepts for understanding human society.

18. Bohannan says there are two general categories of culture: culturized animal behavior and pure culture. Describe the differences between these categories in terms of at least five of the eleven principles of social organization. Then evaluate the usefulness of these two categories for the understanding of human evolution.

Learning
Culture

2

What students should get out of the chapter . . .

First, all culture is learned. There are two ways of leaning culture: learning its subject matter, and experiencing it. As we grow up and grow older, we experience whatever version of culture is in the environment.

Culture is not the same thing as cross-cultural differences. Cultural differences exist because different specific culture is found in different environments. When we experience our culture, it seems a part of the natural world, which we also learn in good part by experience. Therefore, ethnocentrism is built-in because of our learning-through-experience. However, ethnocentrism is a social trap that can cause great difficulties in today's world.

Second, anthropological fieldwork is an attempt to experience another culture, as an adult, at the same time that we learn it. We then describe accurately the culture we have learned and experienced for the benefit of people who can learn it but, because they were not there and did not learn the language, cannot experience it.

Films and Videos

Learning

The Amazing Newborn. 26 min. color. 1975. Penn State Audio-Visual Services. Presents three normal infants from one to seven days of age who are shown reacting to visual, tactile, and auditory stimuli. The infants' capabilities to fixate on objects, have visual preferences, turn their heads in response to the spoken word, mimic, and move their bodies in the rhythm of voices are illustrated. Six different organized patterns of behavior are identified.

Bathing Babies in Three Cultures. 9 min. black and white. 1954. University of California Extension Media Center. Comparative study of the interplay between mother and child in three different settings— the Sepik River in New Guinea, a modern American bathroom, and a mountain village in Bali. Produced by Gregory Bateson and Margaret Mead.

Cross-Cultural Differences in Newborn Behavior. 12 min. black and white. 1974. Penn State Audio-Visual Services. Demonstrates some of the research results obtained from the application of the Cambridge Behavioral and Neurological Assessment Scales to normal newborns in hospital nurseries. Indicates that there are standard differences in temperament or behavior among babies from different ethnic backgrounds—Caucasian, Navajo, Aborigine, African—and that such differences among humans are biological as well as cultural. Produced by Daniel G. Freedman.

Karba's First Years. 19 min. black and white. 1950. University of California Extension Media Center. Scenes in the life of a Balinese child, beginning with his relationships to parents, aunts and uncles, child nurse, and other children, as he is suckled, taught to walk and to dance, teased, and titillated. Illustrates how a Balinese child's responsiveness is muted when parents stimulate and then themselves fail to respond. Anthropologist: Margaret Mead.

Fieldwork

To Find the Baruya Story. 64 min. color. 1982. University of Minnesota. Portrays the work of French anthropologist Maurice Godelier among the Baruya—a tribe famous throughout the east highlands of Papua New Guinea as saltmakers and traders. This film, photographed in both 1969 and 1982, illustrates an anthropologist's actual fieldwork methods and personal relationships among the Baruya, and provides an in-depth view of the Baruya's traditional salt-based economic system.

Chapter 2

Test Items

True/False

1. The abilities to invent tools and use culture are genetic.   T

2. Human infants don't begin to learn culture until two to three months after birth.   F

3. As human children learn their culture, they tend to regard the culture they are learning as part of the natural world.   T

4. The process of learning a first culture is often conscious, while the process of learning a second culture is usually unconscious.   F

5. Two basic problems with the stimulus-response model are that it overemphasizes learning and assumes that all stimuli felt by the animal come from inside.   F

6. The comparator is analogous to a thermostat.   T

7. The process of learning culture is complicated by the fact that people often reevaluate the meanings of their past experiences.   T

8. Schemata are categories for interpreting stimuli.   T

9. Most schemata are not culturally shared, but are unique to one individual.   F

10. Sometimes our schemata keep us from recognizing reality if that reality does not fit our accustomed patterns of perceiving and behaving.   T

11. Most of the choices humans make as they grow are conscious.   F

12. People recognize one or more ideal types of personalities and may try to make their children match those types.   T

13. Stimulus is as important to the very old as it is to the very young.   T

14. Character and social development are complete at the end of adolescence.   F

15. There is no such thing as an unobserved ethnographic fact.   T

16. Ethnography and ethnocentrism are interchangeable anthropological concepts.   F

17. Ethnographers seek to internalize the schemata of the people they are studying.   T

18. The best anthropological fieldwork is marked by a strong lack of self-scrutiny on the part of the researcher.   F

19. Almost all anthropological fieldwork today is carried out in small-scale simple societies.   F

Multiple Choice

1. The process of learning a culture as a child:
    a. is often unconscious
    b. leads to the child regarding that culture as part of the natural world
    c. can become a social trap
    d. is essential for becoming human
    * e. all of the above
    f. ____ and ____

2. Learning more than one culture:
    a. is an unconscious process
    b. can become a social trap
    * c. is the best way to overcome ethnocentrism
    d. all of the above
    e. none of the above

3. The stimulus-response model:
    a. explains all behavior
    * b. leaves out learning
    c. is based on the intentions of the behaving animal
    d. describes a feeling, thinking organism
    e. all of the above
    f. ____ and ____

4. Powers' book *Behavior: The Control of Perception* proposes that:
    a. the stimulus-response model is too limited to explain behavior
    b. an animal is a feedback mechanism
    c. the purpose of any animal's behaving is to allow it to affect and control its stimulus
    d. animals act to bring the actual stimulus they perceive into line with what they wish to perceive
    * e. all of the above
    f. all of the above except ____

5. The comparator:
    a. contains residue from previous experience
    b. is set by culture not genes
    c. weighs a stimulus in terms of both genetic and experiential information
    d. has standards that change
    * e. all of the above except ____ (b)

6. Stimulus:
    a. originates in the external environment
    b. originates in the body
    c. may be perceived by the sense organs
    * d. all of the above
    e. none of the above

7. Schemata:
   - a. are categories for the interpretation of stimuli
   - b. are seldom culturally shared
   - c. bear little relationship to the comparator
   - d. become a permanent part of the way we experience the world
   - e. are useful, but most humans can do without them
   - * f. _____ and _____ (a and d)

8. Most of the choices humans make as they grow:
   - a. are unconscious
   - b. can be circumscribed by culture and by other individuals
   - c. are made by the child from among the available options
   - d. lead to learning that shapes future behavior
   - e. have parameters set by genes and culture
   - * f. all of the above

9. In school, a child learns:
   - a. facts and data necessary for success in a technological society
   - b. to read and write
   - c. that his or her primary task is to identify and fulfill his or her own needs
   - d. to serve the needs of society through learning culturally approved attitudes and behaviors
   - * e. all of above except _____ (c)

10. Ethnocentrism:
   - a. is an attitude that regards one's own group or culture as superior
   - b. sometimes referred to as "naive realism"
   - c. sometimes leads to people branding other cultures as evil
   - d. eliminates the provincialism in our premises and the attitudes that grow from them
   - e. sometimes involves the realization that other peoples are also ethnocentric
   - * f. all of the above except _____ (d)

11. Anthropological fieldworkers:
   - a. must completely keep their personalities out of their work
   - b. can achieve some objectivity through training and practice
   - c. see their status as an alien as an impediment to be overcome
   - d. seek to learn and understand another culture through internalizing its schemata
   - e. try to act as a bridge between cultures
   - * f. all of the above except _____ and _____ (a and c)

12. In the field, emotional discomforts:
   - a. are rare
   - b. provide the best raw material for insights
   - c. offer opportunities for sharpening research skills
   - d. are major impediments to the best kind of objective research
   - e. should be prevented by appropriate training and advance preparation
   - * f. _____ and _____ (b and c)

13. During the fieldwork process, information is elicited:
    a. through learning-by-doing
    b. through participant observation
    c. through asking questions
    d. through interviews and sometimes questionnaires
 * e. all of the above

Essay

1. What does Bohannan mean when he says that to be made human through culture is also to be made provincial?

2. What, according to Bohannan, is the social trap of culture?

3. Explain the differences between the three types of ethnocentrism, and make up a specific example of each type.

4. Explain Bohannan's statement, "All human beings are siblings divided by culture." How did he come to this realization?

5. What inadequacies of the stimulus-response model were resolved by Powers' idea that an animal is a feedback mechanism?

6. Explain the relationship between an organism's genetic deposit in the information bank, its learning deposit, its comparator, and its personal life experience.

7. Explain the concept of "schemata" and discuss its relationship to "the comparator."

8. Why does Bohannan say that anthropologists doing fieldwork must bring their schemata to consciousness?

9. Why do human infants die if they are not stimulated? What are the implications of this fact for the education and healthy development of human young?

10. Explain and evaluate Bohannan's statement, "You are what you do."

11. What do you think of Bohannan's assertion that schools primarily serve the needs, not of children, but of society?

12. Define and discuss the three forms of ethnocentrism, and provide at least one specific example of each.

13. Why must anthropological fieldworkers keep one foot in both cultures?

14. Discuss anthropological fieldwork in terms of Bohannan's metaphor of stereoscopic or binocular vision.

18

Men and Women,
Sex and Babies

3

What students should get out of the chapter . . .

Sex (which is biological), gender (which is cultural), sexuality (which is behavior), and reproduction (which is all of the above) are four different things that should not be confused. The most usual confusion is that between sex and gender, and lies at the basis of genderism (commonly called sexism).

Films and Videos

Gender

Deep Hearts. 53 min. color. 1980. University of California Extension Media Center. Ethnographic documentary on the Bororo Fulani, a nomadic people of the Republic of Niger in Africa. Focuses on a ritual series of dances in which young men compete in a beauty contest. It questions, by implication, what it may mean to be a hostage to culture.

Kypseli: Women and Men Apart—A Divided Reality. 40 min. color. 1976. University of California Extension Media Center. This award-winning ethnographic study of male and female roles in a small Greek village shows how the separation of the sexes and the principle of male dominance have become part of the village's most basic social structure, affecting the daily activities and thoughts of everyone there. Fascinating analysis of a social structure derived from the same cultural heritage shared by all European peoples, and, therefore, of relevance to the study of social patterns and traditional sexual roles in America.

N!ai: The Story of a !Kung Woman. 59 min. color. 1980. Study guide available. Documentary Educational Resources. Told in her own words and song, this poignant film covers twenty-seven years in the life of a !Kung woman from Namibia's Kalahari Desert. Film footage of N!ai's early years, when her small band roamed freely as hunter-gatherers on fifteen thousand square miles, contrasts sharply with her present and vastly different life on a reserve run by the government of South Africa. Recipient of top international awards.

Number Our Days. 29 min. color. 1976. Direct Cinema Ltd. Based on the fieldwork of anthropologist Barbara Myerhoff, this Academy Award winner for best documentary short is a compassionate look at a community of elderly Eastern European Jews living in Venice, California. With sensitivity and patience, the film records the details of the community's life, showing how its members sustain a vivid cultural heritage while contending with poverty and loneliness in modern America.

Rivers of Sand. 83 min. color. 1974. University of California Extension Media Center. Ethnographic study of the Hamar, an isolated people of southwestern Ethiopia, emphasizing the rigidly codified male supremacy upon which the society is organized, and its effects on personal relationships, social roles, and individual behavior. It also considers agricultural and hunting activities, funeral customs, harvest celebrations, and initiation rites for boys entering manhood.

Under the Men's Tree. 15 min. black and white. 1974. University of California Extension Media Center. At Jie cattle camps in Uganda men often gather under a special tree to make leather and wooden goods and to talk, relax, and sleep. The conversation on this particular afternoon becomes a kind of reverse ethnography, centering on the European's most noticeable possession, the motor vehicle. A uniquely delicate and intimate film, filled with the humor of the Jie, and, implicitly, the ironic wit of the filmmakers, David and Judith MacDougall.

Sex

The Mehinacu. 60 min. color. 1974. Films Incorporated Video. Anthropologist Thomas Gregor explores the strikingly ambivalent feelings Mehinacu men and women have for one another in their central Brazilian village. Even different areas of the village are male or female domains and a man who spends too much time in the women's area risks being called "a woman" or "a rubbish-yard man." The mixture of antagonism and affection between the sexes comes to the surface during the annual piqui rituals, the focus of the film. These are designed to insure a good fruit harvest. But the piqui tree in Mehinacu legend grew from the sexual organs of the murdered alligator lover of two Mehinacu girls. This, therefore, sets the tone for the month-long celebrations with their semi-erotic ritual games and dances.

Chapter 3

Test Items

True/False

1. Culture is humans' primary survival strategy.   T

2. In both biological and cultural processes, the male is ultimately concerned with the young for longer periods of time than is the female.   F

3. Males in some societies try to symbolically usurp the female role in reproduction.   T

4. American culture always makes clear distinctions between sex, sexuality, and gender.   F

5. Gender is behavior involving the organs that determine sex.   F

6. Sexual intercourse has been the overwhelmingly privileged expression of sexuality in law, custom, and religion because it is the only technique of sexuality that can result in procreation.   T

7. Reproduction is merely the creation of offspring without the influence of culture.   F

8. Aspects of reproduction include householding and economic activities.   T

9. There is no nonculturized way for humans to express or act out their sexuality.   T

10. There are some societies that grant legitimacy to every possible sexual act.   F

11. American society has been traditionally classified as sexuality-positive.   F

12. The sexual repression on Inis Beag was anchored by religious custom and the fear of gossip.   T

13. Trobriand youngsters are allowed complete sexual freedom until they marry.   T

14. The Mehinaku of Brazil are a rare example of a people with no anxieties about any forms of sexuality.   F

15. Menstruation is purely biological; there are no cultural aspects associated with it.   F

16. Menstrual taboos often work to women's advantage.   T

17. In some societies, men mimic both menstruation and birth in ceremonies designed to make men appear to be more important in the reproductive process.   T

18. The Trobrianders and Aranda believe that men have nothing to do with the physical making of babies.   T

19. According to the Hua, babies are made before birth from the mixing of blood and semen, and after birth from breast milk, sweat and body oils rubbed on the skin.   T

20. People do not maintain nonscientific ideas because mythic social truth is not as important as factual scientific truth.   F

21. The couvade is a created fiction to give men a greater role in the reproductive process.   T

22. Sexuality is important only for procreation.   F

23. The increased availability of contraception was a major contributing factor in the increased sexual permissiveness of American society after 1960.   T

24. Assuming that gender and sexuality must absolutely overlap sets the cultural stage for the persecution of homosexuals. **T**

25. In American and British society, inversion of gender roles sometimes appears to entail political subversion as well. **T**

26. Homosexuality can be usefully thought about as an issue in gender definition. **T**

27. There are no societies in which gender is determined by sex alone; rather, gender is always determined by behavior. **F**

28. In some societies, such as that of Mombasa, homosexuality offers many people a chance for what they define as a better life. **T**

29. The differences between "masculine" and "feminine" are biologically determined. **F**

30. Most complex modern culture can be used by the members of either sex, making the assigning of specific gender roles less necessary and more complex. **T**

31. Male and female infants in American hospitals are treated exactly the same. **F**

32. Gender identity has to do with the social position and cultural tasks that a person is assigned on the basis of sex. **T**

33. Gender identity always involves some degree of personality repression. **T**

34. Men, because they do the heaviest work in all societies, are everywhere thought of as the "back-up" gender. **F**

35. Sex and aggression are hormonally based, and sometimes become confused. **T**

36. Eliminating gender stereotypes and broadening gender role definitions can eliminate enormous waste of brains and talent. **T**

Multiple Choice

1. Biological sex:
   a. is genetically determined
   b. carries an enormous cultural overload
   c. is involved with procreation
   d. is only one of many criteria in any definition of gender
   e. all of the above
   * f. all of the above except _____ (b)

2. Sexual intercourse:
   a. is the only technique of sexuality that can result in procreation
   b. has been the most commonly sanctioned expression of sexuality in law, custom, and religion
   c. includes all important aspects of reproduction
   d. determines gender
   * e. _____ and _____ (a and b)

3. Reproduction:
    a. is just another term for procreation
    b. means sexual intercourse and having babies
    c. includes all the biological and cultural ways of assuring the survival to adulthood of the next generation
    d. has to do with assuring the future of both the group and its culture
    * e. _____ and _____ (c and d)

4. Aspects of reproduction include:
    a. householding and economic activities
    b. sexuality and procreation
    c. the protection and enculturation of the young
    * d. all of the above
    e. all of the above except _____

5. The people of Inis Beag:
    a. engage in an extreme of sexual freedom
    b. have invented clever ways of encouraging sexuality while appearing not to
    c. isolate their women in menstrual huts, reflecting their collective belief in menstruation as polluting
    d. believe that babies are built by substances from the mother's body alone
    * e. none of the above

6. Some human societies:
    a. are very tolerant of extramarital affairs
    b. perceive women as passionless
    c. perceive sexuality as weakening and debilitating to men
    d. allow young unmarried women and men to make love in the woman's mother's hut but don't allow them to eat together before marriage
    * e. all of the above
    f. all of the above except _____

7. Menstrual taboos:
    a. simply reflect men's desire to dominate and control women
    b. sometimes reflect male beliefs in the polluting nature of menstruation
    c. always work to keep women in subordinate positions in society
    d. often work to women's advantage
    * e. _____ and _____ (b and d)

8. About procreation, some societies believe that:
    a. the baby is made from the coagulation of semen and menstrual fluid
    b. the child is contained in the male seed
    c. conception results from sexual intercourse
    * d. all of the above
    e. all of the above except _____

9. The Trobriand Islanders believed that a baby's body is built from physical substances contributed by the mother alone. This belief:
    a. leads to the concomitant belief that the mother reinforces her own substance in the child through nursing
    b. was directly correlated with their principle of matrilineal descent
    c. was completely thrown out after the scientific facts were presented through Western teaching
    d. all of the above
  * e. all of the above except _____ (c)

10. In some societies men reinforce their contribution to the biological dimension of reproduction by:
    a. simulating menstruation
    b. eating foods grown by women
    c. giving boys special medicine to produce semen
    d. avoiding strenuous activity
  * e. all of the above
    f. all of the above except _____

11. Homosexuality:
    a. is sometimes perceived in American and British society as politically subversive
    b. is seen as anomalous in cultures that limit sexuality to procreation
    c. makes the reproductive tasks of rearing children impossible
    d. has been historically persecuted by societies that assume that gender and sexuality must absolutely overlap
    e. all of the above
  * f. all of the above except _____ (c)

12. In some societies, homosexuality:
    a. offers concrete and socially-approved opportunities for economic advancement
    b. is a complex phenomenon associated with turning boys into men and with ritually reinforcing the social world
    c. was the socially-approved norm for all social members
  * d. all of the above
    e. all of the above except _____

13. Caretakers in American hospitals:
    a. tend to treat girl and boy babies exactly alike
    b. raise the pitch of their voices significantly when talking to girls
    c. handle boy babies with larger gestures than they do girls
    d. tend to cuddle boys more than girls
  * e. _____ and _____ (b and c)

14. Gendercentrism reflects:
    a. our individual experiences of being male and female
    b. our reactions to the ways we are dealt with as males and females
    c. what we are taught
    d. stereotypical opinions about gender
 * e. all of the above
    f. none of the above

15. Gender identity:
    a. always involves some degree of personality repression
    b. has to do with social position and cultural tasks assigned on the basis of sex
    c. is formed earlier in life than sex identity
    d. is rendered problematic for many people by narrow cultural definitions of gender-appropriate behavior
    e. all of the above
 * f. all of the above except _____ (c)

16. Eliminating gender stereotypes and narrow definitions of gender-appropriate behavior, according to Bohannan, would:
    a. lead to cultural chaos and disintegration
    b. fly in the face of nature, which clearly predisposes men to do one set of things and women another
 * c. free all the brains and talent of the species to do the total cultural mission
    d. none of the above

Essay

1. In your own words, define sex, sexuality, and gender. Explain why it is important to distinguish among them.

2. Using specific examples, describe the range of human sexual behaviors.

3. What is a doctrine of procreation, and what effects does it have on cultural life? Contrast the Hua doctrine of procreation described by Bohannan with the American version as you yourself understand it. What sort of behaviors does each doctrine encourage? What values does each reflect?

4. Describe a doctrine of procreation most likely to be held by a society that 1) holds women and men to be equal; 2) is extremely male-dominated; 3) values women more than men.

5. Compare and contrast Trobriand, Aranda, and American doctrines of procreation, and explain how each doctrine is embedded in and expressive of its culture.

6. Why does Bohannan say that "Many people in Western society maintain nonscientific ideas even when they know the science, because mythic social truth is as important to them as factual scientific truth (and may be more emotionally and spiritually fulfilling)"? Explain, using your own examples.

7. Describe the institution of couvade, and explain its presence in contemporary American society.

8. Discuss homosexuality in terms of sexuality, gender and culture, using at least two specific examples.

25

9. What does it mean to be gendercentric? Evaluate the usefulness of this concept.

10. Does gendercentrism always take the form of thinking that one's own sex is best? Why or why not?

11. Why does Bohannan call women the "back-up" gender? What does this term imply? Is this term descriptive or appropriate?

12. What major cultural assumptions about gender and childrearing have been recently altered by feminist anthropology?

13. Discuss the relationships between sex, gender and power.

14. What do cultures lose when they define gender narrowly, and what do you think should be done about that?

Marriage and Family

4

What students should get out of the chapter . . .

Marriage is the common human method for legitimizing children, in the sense that they have a full set of kinfolk on both their father's and mother's sides. Marriage usually involves sexual and domestic rights (but there are cases in which it does not). All marriages begin in some method by which spouses find each other, then proceed through developmental phases; all marriages end, either in death of one partner or in divorce.

Families and households are to be distinguished: a family is a kinship group, a household is a local group. The fact that families usually form households must not obscure the difference. Families can be made larger by plural marriage (polygyny and polyandry) and by extension along lineal and collateral lines to include a greater proportion of kinfolk.

Films and Videos

Family

Life Chances. 43 min. black and white. 1970. University of California Extension Media Center. Ethnographic study of four families in a prosperous village in the fertile western plains of Cyprus. Illustrates the impact of social and economic change on the village in the past fifty years, showing how the traditional peasant economy of self-sufficient subsistence production has evolved into a complex market system based on the division of labor. Depicts in detail the lives of several generations in four families descended from a common ancestor in order to demonstrate the complex factors at work in the changing structure of social stratification in the village.

Marriage

Argument About a Marriage. 18 min. color. 1966. Study guide available. Documentary Educational Resources. Documents a conflict between two groups of Bushmen in the Kalahari Desert of southern Africa over the legitimacy of a marriage. The first part uses narration, some stills, and background footage to trace the history of the argument; then the entire conflict is shown, with Bushman voices and a few subtitles. Shot by John Marshall during the Peabody expedition to Africa in 1956.

Rana. 19 min. color. 1976. University of Illinois Film and Video Center. Provides a glimpse into the life and role of women in India. Rana is twenty-one, Muslim and a college student living with her extended family in an overcrowded house of Old Delhi. Daily routine is simple, aided by few modern conveniences, and domestic work is shared among females of the household. Although Rana is a comparatively modern Muslim who puts aside the veil in co-education university classes, her parents still have full responsibility of selecting her husband, and thereby deciding her future.

Tobelo Marriage. 106 min. color. 1990. University of California Extension Media Center. Chronicles a fascinating marriage ritual among the Tobelo of North Halmahera, a Moluccan island of eastern Indonesia. The storyline follows a dispute over a dramatic elopement and wedding that has split the society. It is one of the best film accounts of how the fabric of a society, torn by dispute, is carefully repaired. Includes the various ceremonies associated with the marriage, as well as the preceding negotiations and preparatory activities.

Chapter 4

Test Items

True/False

1. Marriage is a human universal, and marriages everywhere are based on cultural notions of partnership and romantic love. F

2. Marriage in most cultures is carried out through a ritual, legal, or economic event before which (if the parties change their minds) the process can be merely abandoned, but after which a divorce must occur. T

3. Incest taboos in all cultures have to do with forbidding sexual relationships only among members of the nuclear family except between husband and wife. T

4. Rules of exogamy forbid members of a specified social group to marry each other. T

5. Close interbreeding within families has been shown to have no deleterious genetic effects. F

6. Exogamy encourages the exchange of both genes and trade goods between groups. T

7. In almost all cultures, people get acquainted, get married, and set up a household, in that order. F

8. Bridewealth means the purchase of the bride by the groom and his family. F

9. Dowry is a gift of property that accompanies the bride and is intended to be used for her support. T

10. The levirate is a system by which the children of a dead man are cared for by his brother. F

11. Divorce occurs in all known human cultures. F

12. No divorce customs in any society can break the kinship-like relationship between the couple after a child is born. T

13. Some American divorcees are uncomfortable because there is no way of undoing the religious rituals that made the marriage. T

14. Divorce is always simpler than widowhood in most societies. F

15. The family is universal among humans. T

16. The family can do, and does, everything that society requires that is not done by some other social group. T

17. Male baboons remain in their native bands and form dominance hierarchies. F

18. The weakest link in any human family system is the link between father and child. F

19. The members of a household are bound to one another on the basis of shared residence. T

20. Just as animals have herds or colonies, human beings have families grouped in bands or communities. T

21. Households cannot exist when there is no kinship relationship. F

22. In many societies, households are based on the mother-son relationship. F

23. In the institution of groom service, the son-in-law spends several months caring for his father-in-law's horses after marriage.   F

24. Households based on mother-daughter relationships are so complete that males may feel left out and form antisocial groups.   T

25. A recurrent difficulty in a monogamous household is short-handedness.   T

26. Polygyny means marriage to plural men, while polygamy means marriage to plural women.   F

27. The preferred marriage form in the largest number of societies is monogamy.   F

28. Advantages of polygyny for women include the shared labor and companionship of their co-wives, while advantages of polygyny for men include a large number of legitimate offspring.   T

29. Polygyny has few disadvantages for either sex.   F

30. Sororal polygyny means several sisters marrying the same man.   T

31. In polygynous societies, there are usually far more women than men.   F

32. In polyandry, several brothers marry several sisters.   F

33. In the U.S., the statistically dominant household form is built around monogamous marriage and the nuclear family.   F

34. Single-parent households are usually matricentric, seriously understaffed, and often associated with poverty.   T

35. About 30 percent of the children of divorce live with their fathers.   F

36. The household of remarriage can lead to twenty-two different types of relationships.   T

37. Difficulties inherent in stepfamilies could be greatly softened if American society would switch to a matrilocal household form.   T

Multiple Choice

1. Marriage is:
    a. a cultural device by which a society can recognize bonding between a man and woman to make their children legitimate
    b. in most cultures, a partnership based on romantic love
    c. a peculiarly human way of looking at and organizing mating
    d. a political device for linking separate segments of a society together
 * e. all of the above except _____ (b)

2. Rules of exogamy:
    a. state that the members of one group must marry each other
 * b. usually work to encourage trade between groups
    c. determine the age of children at marriage
    d. shape the kind of marriage ceremony performed
    e. all of the above

3. In some cultures:
    a. the specific individual each person is to marry is mandated
    b. marriages are arranged by parents, kinfolk, or matchmakers
    c. people must find each other and make their own matches
    d. everyone must be married all the time
  * e. all of the above
    f. all of the above except _____

4. In some cultures, potential mates:
    a. get acquainted, get married, make love, and set up a household
    b. get married, set up a household, make love, get acquainted
    c. make love, get acquainted, set up a household, get married
    d. make love, get acquainted, get married, set up a household
  * e. all of the above
    f. all of the above except _____

5. Bridewealth is:
    a. the passing of goods from the groom's family to the bride's family
    b. payment for purchase of a bride
    c. a means for repaying the bride's family for rearing her, then losing her
    d. a stabilizing factor of the relationships of in-laws throughout the society
    e. all of the above
  * f. all of the above except _____ (b)

6. The levirate:
    a. is a system that provides for a dead man's children to be cared for by his brother
    b. is an Indian custom that requires a widow to cast herself on her husband's funeral pyre
  * c. is a means of providing for a widow by insuring that she will be married and provided for
     by a kinsman of her dead husband
    d. was a European predecessor to the American system of life insurance
    e. none of the above

7. Divorce:
    a. is more complicated than widowhood in most societies
    b. cannot break the kinship-like relationship between co-parents
    c. is problematic for some Americans because they have no way of undoing the religious rituals
     that made the marriage
    d. approaches 100 percent of marriages among the Muslim Kanuri of Nigeria
  * e. all of the above
    f. all of the above except _____

8. The impact of divorce on the household:
    a. is benign in societies with households based on the husband-wife relationship
    b. is usually devastating in societies with households based on the parent-child relationship
    c. is often benign in societies with households based on the parent-child relationship
    d. is often devastating in societies with households based on the husband-wife relationship
  * e. _____ and _____ (c and d)

31

9. The weakest link in any human family system is the link between:
    a. father and child
    b. mother and child
    c. grandparents and grandchildren
  * d. the mated pair
    e. none of the above

10. In anthropological terms, a family is:
    a. a group of people who live together
  * b. a group of people who recognize an association with each other on the basis of shared biological descent
    c. a group of people that gives each member a place to be
    d. a man, a woman, and their children, who live together
    e. _____ and _____

11. The terms matrilocal, patrilocal, uxorilocal, virilocal, unilocal, neolocal, bilocal, and avunculocal apply to:
    a. types of marriage
    b. age categories
  * c. residence patterns
    d. none of the above

12. The most basic criteria for the division of labor within the household are:
    a. degree of kinship
    b. membership in the nuclear family
    c. difficulty of the task and abilities of the individual
  * d. age and sex
    e. all of the above

13. Polygyny:
    a. is the preferred marriage form in the largest number of societies
    b. means a form of marriage in which several women are all married to one male
    c. is often preferred by men as the best way to assure themselves the greatest number of children
    d. solves the problem in monogamy of not enough people to do the necessary work
  * e. all of the above
    f. all of the above except _____

14. Polygamous households work best when:
    a. all the co-wives like each other
    b. when wives produce less than they cost
  * c. relationships between the co-wives are defined in detail
    d. co-wives slight each other's children
    e. all of the above

15. Polyandry:
    a. is a marriage form in which several men, usually brothers, marry one wife
    b. enables Tibetans to avoid subdivision of their family farms
    c. could be considered a form of birth control
    d. is sometimes combined with polygyny
  * e. all of the above
    f. all of the above except ____

16. According to Bohannan, the emergent household forms in the United States:
    a. represent the continued moral breakdown of American society
    b. exhibit the high degree of social disorganization of contemporary American society
  * c. are part of long-term cultural change
    d. all of the above
    e. none of the above

17. One-parent households:
    a. are seriously understaffed
    b. are usually patricentric
    c. are often connected to poverty
    d. constitute a new family form with needs to which American society has not yet fully adapted
    e. all of the above
  * f. all of the above except ____ (b)

Essay

1. a. What does marriage mean to Americans? To other societies? Give specific examples.
   b. Discuss some of the primary similarities and differences between American notions of marriage and those of more traditional societies.

2. What do incest and exogamy have to do with how women and men find each other? Explain in detail.

3. Define bridewealth, dowry and levirate, and discuss what you think the status of women might be in cultures that exhibit each of these institutions.

4. Discuss the family as a universal cultural institution. Use specific examples to make your points.

5. Reinvent the American family as a cultural institution designed specifically to keep the household stable when spouses divorce.

6. Why, according to Bohannan, is the human family "an organizational miracle"? What are the primary differences between human and animal families?

7. Using specific examples, describe the differences between family and household, and explain why Bohannan sees these differences as "vital."

8. Use specific examples to describe at least three different cornerstone household relationships in terms of the balance of power in such relationships (including who is peripheral and who is not), their stability and continuity, and their ability to adapt to divorce of the mated pair. Which type would you prefer to live in, and why? Would that be possible in contemporary American society?

9. Discuss polygyny as a marriage form. What are its benefits for men? for women? for children? its disadvantages? Would you be willing to live in a polygynous family? Why or why not?

10. Why is polyandry so rare? Why does it exist at all? Evaluate its adaptiveness as a marriage form in the areas in which it is practiced. Might it also be adaptive elsewhere? Explain.

11. Given what you know about the contemporary world, evaluate the relative benefits of monogamy, polygyny, and polyandry. Which form would you personally prefer, and why? If you were assigned to choose the most adaptive form for the future of the entire human species, which one would you choose? Explain your choice.

Kinship and Community

5

What students should get out of the chapter . . .

Kinship is the basis of society, both animal and human. It does not disappear in modern societies, although it has many competitors for people's time and interest. Kinship provides us with basic identity. We are who we are because of our parents and kinfolk, although we may outgrow that basic identity (a few people even manage to hide it completely). Although it is less urgent in a culture like our own, in which we participate in many non-kinship groups and activities based on common interests, kinship nevertheless still forms an important basis for trust. Human life is unthinkable without kinship.

Test Items

Note to instructor: On p. 86 of Chapter 5, the author suggests skipping pages 86 through 97 if you do not wish to engage your students in the nitty-gritty of kinship terminology. Accordingly, the questions addressing those pages are here presented in separate sections, for your convenience.

True/False

1.	Kinship means the culturized understanding of genetic relatedness among people.	T
2.	Kinship is unrelated to other social and cultural institutions.	F
3.	Kinship is important in all societies because it provides a built-in basis for trust.	T
4.	In large-scale societies, kinship is just as important as in small-scale societies.	F
5.	Kinship is always based on biological relatedness.	F
6.	Godparenthood is always dissociated from kinship.	F
7.	Kinship provides effective metaphors for many different types of social relationships.	T
8.	Adoption of a son to be heir by a family that has no children was once common in China.	T
9.	Female prisoners often create fictive kinship systems centered on mother-daughter or homosexual relationships.	T
10.	The pseudofamilies created by female prisoners mirror only the female-female family relationships in the outside world.	F
11.	The major studies of men's prisons in North America have found no quasi-kinship or family organizations at all comparable to those found in women's prisons.	T
12.	The "kith" in "kith and kin" refers to members of a tightly-knit community.	T
13.	Settlement plus interest group equals community just as household plus family equals home.	T
14.	In the developed world, interest groups and settlements are closely linked.	F
15.	Law is a dimension of the modern settlement.	T
16.	Human motherhood involves mostly instinctive behavior.	F
17.	For chimpanzees and other primates, the quality of mothering they receive makes very little difference in the quality of mothering they will provide for their own young.	F
18.	Parenthood shapes the future of a culture through shaping its future culture-bearers.	T

True/False
for pages 86-97

1.	Middle-scale societies use specialized institutions which are an altered form of the kinship principle to do some specialized jobs.	T

2. Everyone agrees that the technicalities of kinship terminology are irrelevant to a good understanding of anthropology.   F

3. Human kinship is far more concerned with biology than with cultural ideas and values.   F

4. Lineal kinfolk are those to whom we are related by direct descent and ascent.   T

5. A parent-child relationship is agnatic if the parent is female.   F

6. An ascendant is any person from whom one is descended.   T

7. Members of a patrilineal chain are descended through a series of uterine relationships.   F

8. Patrilineal chains are common among primates.   F

9. Matrilineal groups contain a woman's sons and their children.   F

10. People with whom we share ascendant kinfolk, but from whom we are not descended, are called collateral kinfolk.   T

11. An affine is a person to whom one is related by descent.   F

12. Consanguine refers to all biologically-related kinfolk.   T

13. Cross cousins are descended from two brothers and two sisters, while parallel cousins are descended from brother and sister.   F

14. Kinship terms can be easily translated from one language to another.   F

15. Lewis Henry Morgan discovered that most cultures use the same kinship classification systems.   F

16. Kinship groups are formally organized groups of people that contain some but not all of an individual's kinfolk.   T

17. An omnilineal descent group is a cognatic group descended from an ancestral ego.   T

18. The most commonly recognized kinship criterion for limiting consanguine groups is the sex of the parent in parent-child relationships.   T

19. Males have uterine descendants; females have agnatic descendants.   F

20. Jural descent is the inheritance of rights and duties, including both the inheritance of property and succession to social position.   T

21. Biological and jural descent must always overlap.   F

22. A unilineal descent group is always a group of agnatic kinfolk based on an ancestral ego.   F

23. A lineage is a type of unilineal descent group in which the genealogical links are known.   T

24. In patrilineal lineages, biological descent is closely associated with jural descent.   T

25. Patrilineal descent systems usually give women a great deal of freedom.   F

26. Matrilineal descent systems are usually found in societies where women are the primary property holders.   F

27. In matrilineal lineages, biological and jural descent are always distinct.   T

28. Jural descent even in matrilineal societies usually runs from a man to his daughter's son.   F

29. Men are the primary holders of property and status in all societies.   T

30. The principle of segmental opposition has to do with the balance of power.   T

31. Lineage systems can be organized through the principle of segmental opposition or the principle of succession to an office.   T

32. In the lineage system of succession to an office all branches at every level are equal.   F

33. In some societies, both matrilineal and patrilineal lineages are recognized.   T

34. The people of agnatic or uterine groups never see themselves in terms of collaterality.   F

35. When the genealogy of a group is not known or is not of vital importance, such a group is most often called a clan.   T

Multiple Choice

1. Kinship:
    a. means the culturized understanding of genetic relatedness
    b. undergirds many political and economic institutions and religious activities
    c. is usually the dominant social principle in small-scale societies
    d. cannot provide an adequate basis for social organization in large-scale societies
    * e. all of the above

2. Adoption:
    a. is only known and practiced in the Western world
    b. is the same as fosterage
    c. is practiced in many societies all over the world
    d. gives nonbiologically-related children the rights and privileges of biological kin
    e. all of the above
    * f. ____ and ____ (c and d)

3. Pseudofamilies created by female prisoners:
    a. create trustworthy and stable small groups in a hostile environment
    b. constitute a kinship system centered around homosexual alliances or fictive mother-daughter relationships
    c. sometimes involve brother-brother and father-son relationships
    d. generally follow outside norms regarding incest prohibitions
    * e. all of the above
    f. all of the above except ____

4. Human communities:
    a. consist of settlements whose members have no common interests
    b. offer companionship, safety, shared labor and subsistence
    c. unlike households, demand no maintenance
    d. have been greatly altered in the industrial and postindustrial worlds
    e. all of the above
    * f. ____ and ____ (b and d)

5. Human mothering behavior:
    a. is instinctive
    * b. is learned
    c. does not affect the behavior of the offspring
    d. only means caring for the bearers of one's genes
    e. all of the above except ____

39

6. Parenting behavior:
   a. has little effect on the psychological development of the young in most cultures
   b. involves support from interest groups
   c. shapes human young as culture-bearers, and thus influences the future directions a given culture will take
   d. all of the above
   * e. all of the above except _____ (a)

Multiple Choice
for pages 86-97

1. Those kinfolk to whom we are related by direct descent and ascent are called:
   a. begotten kinfolk
   b. conceived kinfolk
   c. agnatic kinfolk
   d. uterine kinfolk
   * e. lineal kinfolk

2. Which statement is not true?
   a. A parent-child relationship is agnatic if the parent is male.
   b. An ascendant is any person from whom one is descended.
   * c. A matrilineal chain traces descent through a series of agnatic relationships.
   d. Uterine pertains to the female.
   e. A patrilineal society traces descent through the father-son relationship.

3. Which statement is true?
   a. Matrilineal chains are rare in the animal kingdom.
   b. Patrilineal chains are common among primates.
   c. Matrilineal groups contain a woman's sons and daughters and their children.
   * d. Patrilineal groups contain a father's daughters but exclude their children.
   e. None of the above.

4. Identify the incorrect statement:
   a. Collateral kinfolk are those with whom we share ascendant kinfolk, but from whom we are not descended.
   b. An affine is a person to whom one is related through marriage.
   * c. Affines are always consanguine kinfolk.
   d. Cousins whose parents are two brothers or two sisters are termed parallel cousins.
   e. Uterine relationships are always consanguine.

5. Lewis Henry Morgan:
   a. discovered that the unrelated Iroquois and Ojibwa languages classified kinfolk in the same ways, but very differently from English and Latin classification systems
   b. made a discovery that was important because before that, most people had naively assumed that kinship classifications were not significantly different across cultures
   c. erred in designing his questionnaires based on English kinship terminology
   d. identified the differences between descriptive and classificatory kinship systems
   e. all of the above
   * f. all of the above except _____ (c)

40

6. Kinship groups:
    a. are formally organized groups of people that contain some but not all of a given individual's kinfolk
    b. usually contain affines
    c. are often composed of either agnatic or uterine kinfolk
    d. can be omnilateral, as in the Anglo-Saxon sib
    e. all of the above
  * f. all of the above except _____ (b)

7. Jural descent:
    a. means the inheritance of rights and duties
    b. includes both inheritance of property and succession to social positions
    c. often overlaps with biological descent
    d. differentiates being a son from being an heir
  * e. all of the above
    f. all of the above except _____

8. A unilineal descent group:
    a. could be a group of agnatic kinfolk based on an ancestral ego
    b. could be a group of uterine kinfolk based on an ancestral ego
    c. is always a group in which descent is considered by members to be the most important point
    d. is always a group in which collaterality is considered by members of the group to be the most important point
    e. all of the above
  * f. all of the above except _____ (d)

9. Patrilineal lineages:
    a. are unilineal descent groups in which the genealogical linkages are known
    b. are agnatic
    c. usually involve close parallels between biological and jural descent
    d. sometimes restrict women severely in order to guarantee a blood tie between father and son
  * e. all of the above
    f. all of the above except _____

10. Matrilineal lineages:
    a. usually involve close parallels between biological and jural descent
    b. are always found in societies in which women are the primary holders of property
  * c. usually run jural descent from a man to his sister's son
    d. are generally found in societies highly restrictive of women
    e. all of the above except _____
    f. none of the above

Essay

1. Compare and contrast the role of kinship in small- and large-scale societies.

2. Discuss kinship as a metaphor. Use specific examples from several cultures, both from your readings and from personal experience.

3. Why do prisoners create pseudofamilies? Do both male and female prisoners do this in the same ways? Explain and describe.

4. Explain the relationships of settlements, households, kith and kin, and interest groups to communities, providing specific examples.

5. What do mothering and fathering have to do with instinct? with learning? with the psychological development of the child? with the future of a culture? Why does the quality of parenting matter?

Essay
for pages 86-97

1. Define the following terms: agnatic, uterine, affine, collateral, consanguine, matrilineal and patrilineal. Explain their interrelationships and their uses in anthropological analyses of kinship.

2. What does Bohannan mean when he says that kinship terms are "role tags"? Discuss the relationship between kinship classifications and behavior, using specific examples.

3. What was important about Lewis Henry Morgan's work with kinship systems?

4. What are lineages? How are they organized? What purposes do they serve?

5. *Using as many kinship terms and categories from Chapter 5 as possible*, diagram the kinship system of your own family.

Part Two

CUMULATIVE ESSAY QUESTIONS

1. Invent a human culture that does not currently exist. Describe its doctrine of procreation, and design its systems for marriage, family, kinship, inheritance and incest prohibition, using specific anthropological labels to describe the characteristics of each system. Explain how each system will affect gender relations, parent-child relations, and household and community structure.

2. Pick two human cultures with very different kinship systems and compare and contrast them in terms of: marriage, family structure, household organization, lineage system, inheritance, and gender and parent-child relations.

3. Consider how your own family would be affected by some of the characteristics of families in other cultures. What would be the benefits? What aspects would be the most disturbing? Why?

Bread and Work

6

What students should get out of the chapter . . .

Western economy, based on the system of capitalism, has turned work into labor, wealth into capital, resources into "land," and ingenuity into entrepreneurship. All four of these features enter the same market as products. This is a most unusual (indeed, alien) arrangement in world history and world ethnology. Redistribution and reciprocity are other methods for distributing goods and services. Work is a major determinant of gender and status in all the world's societies; the kind of work varies with ecological base and economic organization.

Films and Videos

Ecology

The Buffalo Creek Flood: An Act of Man. 40 min. black and white. 1975. University of Minnesota. On February 26, 1972, a giant coal waste dam at the head of a hollow in Logan County, West Virginia, burst, sweeping 130 million gallons of water down the crowded valley of Buffalo Creek. One hundred twenty-four people were killed, four thousand left homeless. Officials of the Pittston Company, owners of the dam, described the disaster as "an act of God." The film intercuts scenes of the devastation with interviews with survivors, union and citizens' group representatives, and the president of the coal company to document how and why such a disaster was allowed to occur.

The Turtle People. 26 min. color. 1973. University of California Extension Media Center. Ethnographic study of the Miskito Indians of eastern Nicaragua, showing how the world demand for turtle meat—once their primary food source—has disrupted their traditional economy and ecology. Documents how the Miskito have entered the world market economy, and demonstrates that since the turtles have become a commercial commodity rather than a subsistence resource their exploitation has increased so greatly that they are now in danger of extinction.

Economy

Aegean Sponge Divers. 27 min. color. 1974. University of California Extension Media Center. Ethnographic documentary on the Greek sponge fishermen of Kalymnos Island. Shows the daily activities of villagers, then focuses on the divers, demonstrating how their rigid code of masculinity pressures them into ignoring basic safety precautions.

Exchange

The Feast. 29 min. color. 1970. University of California Extension Media Center. Shows a day-long feast held to begin the formation of an alliance between two southern Venezuelan Yanomamö Indian villages. Uses narration and still photographs to outline events and designate important persons, then shows (with subtitles and no narration) the feast itself.

The Feast in Dream Village. 27 min. color. 1989. University of California Extension Media Center. Documents a ritual feast in a small village on Sumba, the last Indonesian island with a pagan majority. Shows the preparations for the feast, the invocations of the spirits, and the performances of numerous sacred rituals. Focuses, however, on the conflict that develops between the head priest and the feast's sponsor over who will maintain control and authority over the ceremonies.

Herding

The Nuer. 75 min. color. 1971. University of California Extension Media Center. Depicts, with minimum of narration, the harmony and rhythm of the present-day dry season life of the Nuer, a people native to Ethiopia and the Sudan. Shows them caring for their cattle and training their young warriors, and captures the subtle patterns of their collective interaction in work, play, and ritual.

Horticulture

Dani Sweet Potatoes. 19 min. color. 1974. University of California Extension Media Center. Illustrates the sophisticated sweet potato horticulture of the Dani people in New Guinea, showing the clearing and burning of fallow brush, scooping fertile mud from irrigation ditches, and planting and cooking the sweet potatoes.

Hunting and Gathering

The Hunters. 72 min. color. 1976. Films Incorporated Video. This classic film documents the primitive tribal culture of the Bushmen of the Kalahari Desert in southwest Africa. It follows four men through a thirteen-day giraffe hunt, carefully delineating each character while recording all phases of the hunt—preparations, trailing the wounded animal, the kill, dividing the meat, and relating the adventure to the tribe. Shot by John Marshall during the Peabody Expedition to Africa in 1956.

Chapter 6
Test Items

True/False

1. Most people tend to exploit all of the resources in their environment in order to get their living. **F**

2. Human use of only a few resources usually works to stabilize a given environment. **F**

3. Work means what people do in order to use resources to allow survival and prosperity. **T**

4. In hunting-gathering societies, the primary division of labor is that between the older and younger generations. **F**

5. Types of labor can be divided and subdivided without much affecting social organization. **F**

6. In industrial society, play/work is often confused with pleasure/pain. **T**

7. Many peoples of the world contrast work with laziness rather than with play. **T**

8. Industrial societies place higher value on work paid with money than on work done for maintenance or subsistence. **T**

9. The labor value of subsistence and maintenance work is computed into the American gross national product (GNP). **F**

10. Hunting-gatherering provides the poorest and most difficult life of all subsistence types. **F**

11. Hunting and gathering cultures have been extinct for centuries. **F**

12. Among foragers, women play an important role in subsistence. **T**

13. Caring for the herd is primarily the responsibility of women. **F**

14. People who live in herding societies tend to accumulate many material possessions. **F**

15. Most pastoral societies are either nomadic or transhumant. **T**

16. The ancient Hebrews described in the first five books of the Bible were hunter-gatherers. **F**

17. Horticulture involves gardening with hand tools such as the digging stick and the hoe. **T**

18. Women play a role in horticultural societies similar to the one they play in pastoral societies. **F**

19. Horticulture allows for a much denser population than foraging or herding. **T**

20. It is likely that women were the first to engage in horticulture as an extension of their gathering activities. **T**

21. The human lifestyle that is the most ecologically balanced and that has been around the longest is hunting-gathering. **T**

22. The Tiv, with whom Bohannan worked, use plow agriculture. **F**

23. The Industrial Age is traditionally dated from the invention of the automobile. **F**

24. Factory industrialism separated the spheres of work and home on a wide scale for the first time in human history. **T**

47

25. Industrial production gives rise to new sets of values but has little effect on the structure of the community.   **F**

26. Women's roles in the industrial world were radically redefined.   **T**

27. The early labor unions included women, and worked to get them equal pay with men.   **F**

28. Industrial society is the opposite of hunting-gathering in that it removes the household as the basic production unit.   **T**

29. In the contemporary developed world, fewer and fewer people are being employed in industrial production.   **T**

30. Ecology is the study of the interrelationships between living things and their environments.   **T**

31. Humans use culture to bend the environment to their own needs.   **T**

32. Agriculture has been proven to do very little environmental damage.   **F**

33. Contemporary peoples are more efficient at ruining the environment than their predecessors.   **T**

34. The task of ecological anthropology is to discover what kinds of damage to the environment are created by different kinds of culture.   **T**

35. Every economy involves the production, distribution, and consumption of goods and services.   **T**

36. Land in all cultures is considered a commodity that can be bought and sold.   **F**

37. Money is one of the great simplifying inventions of all time.   **T**

38. Householding, reciprocity, redistribution, and market are the four basic modes of the allocation of goods and services in cultures.   **T**

39. Householding means ownership of private housing.   **F**

40. Redistribution involves the exchange of goods between people who are already associated with one another.   **F**

41. Reciprocity means that goods and services flow into a central point and are then reallocated by authorities.   **F**

42. The market principle always dominates in societies that have a marketplace.   **F**

43. Capitalist systems exhibit the creation and maintenance of a permanent underclass.   **T**

44. In *kula* exchange, one gets the most prestige by obtaining a valuable and keeping it.   **T**

45. The market principle is the only economic principle so far discovered that can successfully run a complex and elaborate industrial economy.   **T**

Multiple Choice

1. Humans:
    a. tend to systematically exploit almost all of the resources in a given environment
    b. often enhance the environmental balance through full resource utilization
    c. often rely on only a few key resources
    d. tend to upset the environmental balance through cultural conservatism
  * e. _____ and _____ (c and d)

48

2. Work:
    a. in simple societies is most basically divided between women and men
    b. has to do with resource utilization
    c. has little to do with social organization
    d. is contrasted with play in most cultures
    e. all of the above
  * f. _____ and _____ (a and b)

3. Industrial societies:
    a. contrast productive with nonproductive work
    b. place highest value on the productive work of maintenance and subsistence
    c. place highest value on work paid with money
    d. consider subsistence and maintenance work to be part of the gross national product
  * e. _____ and _____ (a and c)

4. Hunting and gathering subsistence:
    a. is more difficult and less productive than agriculture
    b. supports large numbers of people in a society
    c. rarely includes reciprocal gift giving
  * d. combines the basic units of production and consumption
    e. all of the above

5. Herding societies:
    a. tend to be egalitarian in terms of gender relations
    b. place women in a lower social position than any other subsistence type
    c. allow a greater density of population than hunting and gathering
    d. are almost always nomadic or transhumant
  * e. all of the above except _____ (a)

6. In horticultural societies:
    a. women play an extremely important role
    b. fields must be cleared anew every few years
    c. people must work hard for subsistence
    d. people garden with hand tools like the digging stick and the hoe
  * e. all of the above
    f. all of the above except _____

7. Plow agriculture:
    a. allows for enormous population density compared to horticulture and hunting-gathering
    b. requires far more labor than foraging, herding or horticulture
    c. tends to make women more dependent on men than horticulture or foraging, and so often reduces their status
    d. involves the use of the plow, irrigation, fertilizer and animals
  * e. all of the above
    f. all of the above except _____

8. Factory industrialism:
   a. is traditionally dated from the invention of the modern steam engine in 1769
   b. was the first subsistence form to separate the workplace from home and neighborhood
   c. fundamentally changed the definition of women's work and the ideals of femininity, allowing women much power and status in the wider society
   d. sharply reduced the proportion of the population engaged in producing basic foodstuffs
   e. all of the above
 * f. all of the above except _____ (c)

9. In the contemporary service society:
   a. industrial production is increasingly being moved to the Third World
   b. more and more people are performing services than making goods
   c. presentation of self is often as important as quality of work
   d. the status of women is further declining
   e. all of the above
 * f. all of the above except _____ (d)

10. The environment:
    a. has been carefully protected by all earlier nonindustrial peoples
 * b. has been ravaged by many different cultures throughout human history
    c. is not relevant to the study of cultural anthropology
    d. was systematically protected by the invention of plow agriculture
    e. _____ and _____

11. Industrial society:
    a. has consistently worked to protect the environment with a focus on long-term benefits
 * b. has generally focused on short-term successes without regard for their long-term environmental impact
    c. has little to do with ecological anthropology
    d. is a major focus of the discipline of economic anthropology
    e. _____ and _____

12. The economy:
    a. involves the production, distribution, and consumption of goods and services
    b. has to do with the ways in which people organize themselves to make a living
    c. is a concept irrelevant to the study of simpler societies
    d. is always based on the free market, a special form of the cost-benefit principle
    e. all of the above
 * f. _____ and _____ (a and b)

13. The four economic elements necessary for production to take place include:
    a. land, labor, subsistence, and food
    b. labor, land, capitalism, and entrepreneurship
 * c. labor, land, entrepreneurship, capital
    d. labor, ingenuity, risk taking, and ownership

14. In some human societies:

    a. land is divided into fixed parcels and owned by people

    b. land is not divided and not owned

    c. people's rights to certain pieces of land are in constant flux

    d. land is organized in relation to religious sites

  * e. all of the above

    f. ____ and ____

15. Money:

    a. is one of the great simplifying inventions of all time

    b. is a means for evaluating many different kinds of goods on a common scale

    c. is a far more complicated means of exchange than barter

    d. is a means for the payment of debt

    e. all of the above

  * f. all of the above except ____ (c)

16. The four basic modes of allocation of goods and services are:

    a. householding, capitalism, communism, and socialism

    b. redistribution, taxation, capitalization, and entrepreneurship

  * c. householding, reciprocity, redistribution, and the market

    d. hunting and gathering, agriculture, pastoralism, and horticulture

17. Redistribution involves:

    a. the exchange of goods between people already associated with each other

  * b. the systematic movement of wealth toward an administrative center and its realloca-
tion by authorities.

    c. the exchange of goods at prices determined by the law of supply and demand

    d. the ranking of exchangeable goods in two or more mutually exclusive spheres

18. Reciprocity:

    a. involves exchanges of goods between people already associated with each other

    b. could be said to be encapsulated in the saying, "You scratch my back, and I'll scratch
yours"

    c. is visible in the American economy in the form of gift exchange

    d. is the principle behind the Trobriand institution of *kula*

  * e. all of the above

    f. all of the above except ____

19. A capitalist economy:

    a. is fundamentally based on the principle of redistribution

  * b. necessarily depends on the creation and maintenance of a permanent underclass

    c. gives householding a central economic role

    d. implies government ownership of the means of production

20. Potlatch:

  * a. is a conversion of one category of goods into a higher, more prestigious, category

    b. is a feast held by the Tiv to celebrate marriage exchanges

    c. involves a highly elaborate form of *kula* exchange

    d. takes place in the Trobriand Islands

    e. all of the above

Essay

1. Bohannan points out that in industrial societies, the dichotomy work/play is often confused with pain/pleasure. What do you think he means? What does this tell us about industrial culture? How do its perceptions of work differ from those of other cultures?

2. a. Discuss the three types of work in capitalist society, and explain their relative social value. Give specific examples of each.

    b. Now explain how this differential valuation has affected the status of women.

3. a. Describe the six basic modes of subsistence described by Bohannan. Which type would you prefer to live in? Why?

    b. Evaluate each subsistence mode in terms of its likely effects on the environment. Which are most environmentally sound? Which are most destructive?

4. Compare and contrast hunting-gathering, pastoralism, horticulture, and agriculture in terms of women's roles and status. In each case, discuss the contribution of women to subsistence, and explain the relationship of that contribution to the status women hold relative to men.

5. How does the economic system of a given culture relate to the environment? Discuss, using specific examples.

6. Is land ownership common to all cultures? Explain, using specific examples.

7. a. Describe the four basic modes of allocation of goods and services. Give specific examples of each.

    b. Show how each of these modes exists in American society, using examples, where possible, from your own family life.

8. Correlate the four basic modes of the distribution of goods and services with subsistence strategy as best you can. (For example, which mode do you think was most common among hunter-gatherers? Why? Among horticulturalists? Why? etc.)

9. What do the *kula* and the potlatch have in common? What economic principle(s) of the allocation of goods and services do they represent?

10. What are the advantages of the market principle? the disadvantages? Is this principle at work in the economies of all societies? Explain, using specific examples.

11. Consider Bohannan's question, "How do we get the economic advantages of capitalism at the same time that we find solutions to the problems that capitalism creates?" What are these advantages? What are the problems? Using what you have learned about culture, suggest some creative answers of your own to Bohannan's question.

Conflict
and Order

7

What students should get out of the chapter . . .

Power is manifest in all social situations. The capacity to wield power is based on aggressive energy—which might be called the energy necessary to survive. Aggressive energy can also, obviously, be used for anti-social (i.e., anti-survival) purposes. Social orders that exhibit cultural control of the power so as not to deny the energy are at the basis of legal and political action. A society can be judged on the basis of its capacity to control conflict (which is not the same thing as aggression). War occurs only when culture is inadequate to solve conflict problems any other way.

Films and Videos

The Ax Fight. 30 min. color. 1977. Study guide available. Documentary Educational Resources. Illustrates various ways in which anthropologists can interpret events—in this case an ax fight between men from two Yanomamö Indian villages in southern Venezuela. Shows the same fight four times: first unedited; then edited and with an explanation of what takes place; a third time with an analysis of the action in terms of the kinship of the participants; and, finally, without commentary. Shows that the significance of such an incident can be complex and multifaceted. Shot by anthropologists Timothy Asch and Napoleon Chagnon.

The Battle of Culloden. 72 min. black and white. 1966. Films Incorporated Video. Brilliant, objective reenactment, based on authentic documentation and filmed on Culloden Moor, of the historic battle in 1746 that ended the cause of Bonnie Prince Charlie, his Jacobite rebellion, and the Royal House of Stuart. Shows in detail the heroics, horror, and stupidity of battle; the slaughter of the ancient highland clans by superior English forces; and the military incompetence of the Scottish prince. It ends with the ruthless "pacification" of the Highlands by British, Scots, and Hessians—years that scourged Scotland and destroyed the ancient Highlands way of life. Directed by Peter Watkins for the BBC.

The Cows of Dolo Ken Paye: Resolving Conflict among the Kpelle. 32 min. color. 1970. University of California Extension Media Center. Ethnographic document of the methods of conflict resolution in a village of Kpelle farmers in Liberia. Shows how a trial by ordeal of hot knives is used to solve the mystery of who killed a grazing cow. Also examines the political and economic organization of the Kpelle that underlies the conflict, explaining that only the rich own cattle, which graze upon and destroy the rice crops on which the poor farmers depend for survival. Informative view of contradictory forces at work in a culture in the midst of modernization.

Dead Birds. 83 min. color. 1963. University of California Extension Media Center. Intensive two-year ethnographic study which documents the way of life of the Dani of New Guinea. The Dani base their values on an elaborate system of intertribal warfare and revenge. Clans engage in formal battles and are constantly on guard against raiding parties. When a warrior is killed, the victors celebrate and the victims plan revenge. There is no thought in the Dani world of wars ever ending; without them there would be no way to satisfy the ghosts of the dead. Wars also keep a sort of terrible harmony in a life that otherwise would be hard and dull.

The Mursi. 60 min. color. 1975. Films Incorporated Video. The Mursi of Ethiopia practice a remarkable form of democracy. A tribe without chiefs and leaders, all their decisions are reached in full tribal debate where each warrior who wishes to speak is heard patiently, without interruption or argument, until all the important views and issues have been raised, and a common, unanimous will emerges and action is taken. There is no voting. This film concentrates on how the tribe reaches a life or death decision about how to react to peace proposals from their neighbors, the Bodi.

To Make the Balance. 33 min. black and white. 1970. University of California Extension Media Center. "To make the balance" is a translation of a phrase used to signify government procedures in a Zapotec community in southern Mexico where their unwritten village legal system has few formalities. The system resolves conflict by minimizing the sense of injustice felt by the parties to a case. The law is a style of compromise, equality, de-escalation at all costs—balance. Candid photography shows the *presidente*, an elected court official, handling five disputes. The narrator interprets for the audience as the *presidente* scolds, gives advice, and offers short discourses on duty, marriage, and property rights.

Chapter 7

Test Items

True/False

1. Authority involves the recognition of the power of an individual or an office by others. **T**

2. There is a power structure in all social groups. **T**

3. According to ethologists, aggression is a physiological drive fired by adrenalin. **T**

4. The aggressive drive has been adaptive for human evolution. **T**

5. Agonism is an ethological term for the pain experienced during primate fighting. **F**

6. The aggressive drive can only be expressed in aggressive behavior potentially leading to conflict. **F**

7. Conflict is the opposite of order. **F**

8. Cultures without conflict have been common in human history. **F**

9. Human territoriality is unrelated to animal territoriality. **F**

10. Territoriality and hierarchy are social systems exhibited by nonhuman species for achieving conflict control. **T**

11. Order is the necessary ingredient to reconcile competing interests and allow society to thrive. **T**

12. Humans are more likely to use territoriality than hierarchy to protect themselves and assure their own survival. **F**

13. Only male primates form hierarchies of dominance and submission. **F**

14. Peace is a dynamic state of controlled conflict. **T**

15. Political systems result from the culturization of conflict and peace. **T**

16. Winning a physical fight can trigger physiological sensations of well-being or elation, while losing can lead to hormonal or psychological depression. **T**

17. Crime is a good indicator of where the tensions in a society are located. **T**

18. Some degree of crime probably exists in all human cultures. **T**

19. Drastically reducing crime in the U.S. would require major alterations in American society that many people are not willing to undertake. **T**

20. Riots generally express displaced rage. **T**

21. The primary concern of the Zapotec system of justice is to identify and punish the wrongdoer. **F**

22. Societies generally resolve internal conflicts by diplomacy, and external conflicts by law. **F**

23. Some Native American cultures prize harmony more than warriorhood, while others prize aggression above harmony. **T**

24. The Hopewell Baptists are an example of a conflict-ridden, physically aggressive fundamentalist religious group. **F**

25. A norm is a standard for behavior within a certain group.   **T**

26. Legal institutions involve the recontexting of social norms.   **T**

27. Counteractions and corrections follow the re-establishment of social order in legal systems.   **F**

28. Among the Nuer, being a good fighter was considered the equivalent of being a virtuous man.   **T**

29. Legal systems that rely on self-help are likely to be prone to settling disputes through the courts.   **F**

30. The ordeal was based on the premise that God would not allow an innocent person to be harmed.   **T**

31. Techniques of conflict resolution rarely if ever involve fun and games.   **F**

32. Mediators are usually successful because they can use their positions of authority and power to back up their decisions.   **F**

33. A moot is a group of people organized to discuss matters but not to reconcile them.   **F**

34. Courts are sophisticated legal institutions that only exist in the Western world.   **F**

35. Courts with the authority to see that their decisions are carried out cannot exist without the presence of a state organization.   **T**

36. Societies in which no disputes are allowed to arise usually are governed by dictators.   **T**

37. Dictatorships usually allow open discussion of conflicting points of view, but not disputes.   **F**

38. Social groups that rely on self-help have the advantage of having no limitations on their size.   **F**

39. A "bicentric dictatorship" would be a contradiction in terms.   **T**

40. The American political system is strictly bicentric.   **F**

41. From an anthropological perspective, the first task of diplomacy is translation between cultural idioms.   **T**

42. On Planet Earth, international law is enforced by a unicentric system of government.   **F**

43. Threat of war is a complex form of self-help.   **T**

44. The lack of established institutions for conflict resolution with the authority and clout to enforce their decisions led to the decline of the Greek city-states, but is not a problem in the contemporary world.   **F**

Multiple Choice

1. Authority:
    a. may inhere in individuals
    b. involves the recognition of one person's power by others
    c. is likely to inhere in roles or offices
    d. only appears in complex societies
    e. all of the above
    * f. all of the above except _____ (d)

2. Power:
     a. is structured into all social groups
     b. is the capacity to alter a thing in the environment or the behavior of an individual
     c. often derives from aggression or its threat
     d. in social relationships can imply inequality
 * e. all of the above
     f. all of the above except ____

3. The aggressive drive:
     a. is fired by the hormone adrenalin
     b. has slowed the course of human evolution by making survival more difficult
     c. has been of great adaptive advantage in human evolution
     d. always leads to conflict or the appearance of conflict
     e. all of the above
 * f. ____ and ____ (a and c)

4. Peace is:
     a. a Utopian state of total harmony
     b. the opposite of chaos
 * c. a state of affairs in which conflict between groups is adequately controlled
     d. a balance between territoriality and hierarchy
     e. none of the above

5. Two social principles utilized by primates for the maintenance of order are:
     a. dominance and submission
     b. privacy and ownership
     c. aggressive behavior and the aggressive drive
     d. conflict and aggression
 * e. territoriality and hierarchy

6. Human political systems:
     a. involve the culturization of conflict and peace
     b. are usually interlinked with moral and religious ideas
     c. are systems of power relationships
     d. work to maintain order within the community and protect it against outsiders
 * e. all of the above
     f. all of the above except ____

7. Conflict:
     a. always results in a physical struggle
     b. usually results from at least four conflicting parties
     c. never occurs in religious contexts
 * d. sometimes occurs when the opposing forces are ideas
     e. all of the above

8. Crime:
   a. is a good indicator of where the tensions in a society are to be found
   b. often demonstrates that some individuals are blocked by the social system from reaching culturally valued goals through culturally acceptable means
   c. is an act that is considered wrong by all societies
   d. exists only in poor societies
   e. all of the above
   * f. ____ and ____ (a and b)

9. Significantly reducing crime in the U.S.:
   a. is a completely impossible task
   * b. may require massive structural alterations in American society that many Americans are unwilling to make
   c. will be a fairly easy task if enough money is devoted to law enforcement
   d. would require a switch to a bicentric mode of government

10. Techniques and social institutions for managing conflict include:
    a. confrontation and adversarial action
    b. avoiding and denying the existence of differences
    c. diplomacy, law, and arbitration
    d. joking
    * e. all of the above
    f. ____ and ____

11. The primary concern of the Zapotec system of justice is:
    a. to punish transgressors
    b. to identify the crime
    * c. to restore social balance and harmony
    d. to recompense the victim
    e. to recover the lost or stolen property

12. Norms are:
    a. cultural guides to action
    b. standards for behavior within a certain group
    c. customs, ethical precepts, morals, or manners
    d. what people in a given society always do
    e. all of the above
    * f. all of the above except ____ (d)

13. Law is marked by the following criteria:
    a. it recontexts ideas from other areas of social life
    b. it creates reformulations of customs within culture
    c. it has a set of known sanctions
    d. its sources are found in the customs of other institutions of society
    * e. all of the above
    f. all of the above except ____

14. When norms are broken by deviant social acts:
    a. society always attempts to "right" the wrong
    b. legal institutions guarantee that the breach will be countered
    c. in our society, police often become involved in countering the breach
    d. chain reactions sometimes result
    e. all of the above
    * f. ____ and ____ (c and d)

15. A third set of activities that follows a breach of norm is:
    a. establishing a new status quo
    b. making the action be performed again in accordance with the norm
    c. punishment
    d. returning to status quo
    * e. all of the above
    f. ____ and ____

16. A moot is:
    a. a point that has become irrelevant
    b. a mechanism for conflict resolution
    c. a kind of town meeting
    d. a legal institution originally developed in China
    e. all of the above
    * f. ____ and ____ (b and c)

17. Courts:
    * a. require the presence of a state organization with the authority to see that their decisions are carried out
    b. do not exist in Africa
    c. were common among the Eskimo
    d. rely primarily on mediation and ordeal for successful conflict resolution
    e. none of the above

18. The major tasks of any political system include:
    a. the invention of ever-improving subsistence strategies
    b. primary focus on the enhancement of individual creativity and happiness
    c. the preservation and restoration of order in society
    d. protection of society from external foes
    e. all of the above
    * f. ____ and ____ (c and d)

19. Dictatorships:
    a. usually allow open discussion of conflicts, but quash dispute
    b. occur when the people in power encourage disputing
    * c. are likely to quash both dispute and discussion in the name of maintaining order
    d. generally encourage people to rely on self-help to settle disputes

20. Polities that allow discussion and dispute so that better solutions to social problems can emerge, while at the same time maintaining enough control to allow orderly life, can be said to have:
    a. a self-help orientation
    b. an exclusively bicentric governmental mode
    c. a unicentric governmental mode
  * d. good-enough government

21. The U.S. is governed in:
    a. a unicentric mode
    b. a bicentric mode
    c. a multicentric mode
  * d. both unicentric and bicentric modes

22. In a unicentric political mode:
    a. law is the principal sanction
    b. discussion is central
    c. the breach which sets off the action chain is subject to more than one interpretation
  * d. police are used to keep order
    e. all of the above
    f. ____ and ____

23. A sovereign state:
    a. has two sets of officials
    b. never involves itself with another sovereign state
  * c. may consist of many social groups or subcultures
    d. considers itself equal to other powers within its geographical area
    e. all of the above

24. According to Bohannan, the first task of diplomacy is:
    a. mediation
    b. arbitration
  * c. translation
    d. discussion
    e. none of the above

25. An example of the results of the failure to develop institutions with enough clout to resolve disputes successfully can be found in:
    a. the decline of the ancient Greek city-states
    b. warfare between contemporary nations
    c. the secession of the Southern states and the ensuing Civil War
    d. medieval trial by battle
    e. all of the above
  * f. all of the above except ____ (d)

Essay

1. Discuss the relationships between conflict, order, chaos, harmony, and peace in human societies and in the animal world.

2. Explain the relationship of territoriality and hierarchy to conflict.

3. Why don't humans simply resolve all conflicts through physical fights? Describe as many techniques and social institutions that you can think of (other than physical fighting) which are designed to resolve conflict, and evaluate their relative efficacy.

4. Describe the Zapotec system of justice. What are its central concerns? How do they differ from the central concerns of the American judicial system?

5. Explain the sequence: breach of norm, counteraction, correction, using at least two specific examples from your own experience. What does this sequence have to do with legal institutions?

6. Discuss law in relationship to culture and to Bohannan's notion of "recontexting."

7. What was the point of the ordeal? Why was it used in so many different places and periods to resolve conflicts? How does it compare to our modern jury system in terms of fairness and efficacy?

8. Invent a dispute between two parties in any culture you like, real or imaginary. Then play mediator, and resolve it to the satisfaction of both. What can you conclude about the advantages and disadvantages of the mediating process?

9. Invent a dispute and solve it in the manner of the Nuer, the Zapotecs, and the Hopewell Baptists.

10. a. Consider the relative advantages and disadvantages of the unicentric and bicentric modes of government. Use specific examples to illustrate your points. What seems to you to work best?

    b. Now think about the relations between nations. How are conflicts between sovereign states presently resolved? Given what you know about unicentric, bicentric, and multicentric modes, what might work better?

11. What does warfare between nations have in common with self-help political systems and bicentric modes of government? Extrapolate from your conclusions: What other techniques might two nations utilize for conflict resolution? What would be necessary to insure that these techniques would be successful without war?

Getting
Control

8

What students should get out of the chapter . . .

There are two basic political jobs: managing conflict within the group and maintaining the integrity of the social group against outsiders. Government is any organization that does these jobs. Simple and small-scale governments can be adequately run by families, by religious groups, lineages or ramages, or by big men. The state is a specialized institution—a social invention—for doing these jobs. Once in place, the state may assume, or be assigned, other jobs.

Films and Videos

Fiji: Great Council of Chiefs. 30 min. color. 1980. Brigham Young University. Documents the first meeting of the Great Council of Chiefs in nearly one hundred years. Shows events surrounding preparation for the meeting (food preparation, dance practice, reception of visitors); reception of the Governor-General; and briefly notes the deliberations and decisions of the Council.

Chapter 8

Test Items

True/False

1. Government and state are one and the same.   F

2. In stateless societies, hierarchy is permanently institutionalized.   F

3. The matrilineal Navajo have an egalitarian society in which leadership is a personal quality based on ability and the requirements of the moment.   T

4. The governmental systems of some societies are closely integrated with their ritual and ceremonial cycles.   T

5. In the Hopi kachina cult, the ancestors are impersonated by masked dancers.   T

6. Lineage systems determine kinship roles but are hardly ever associated with government.   F

7. Where lineage systems are in effect, they work to determine who fights with whom.   T

8. Lineage systems can be an effective mode of performing the tasks of government in the absence of a state.   T

9. The principle of equality underlies the principle of segmental opposition.   T

10. Ramages involve lineages that are strictly equal in social status and prestige.   F

11. The ramage constitutes a step toward the evolution of the state.   T

12. The state requires social inequality.   T

13. Melanesian big men are inheritors of offices passed down through the Melanesian lineage system.   F

14. The big man system is associated with the subsistence strategy called redistribution.   T

15. The big man system provides unlimited opportunity for political growth and development.   F

16. While the big man system relies on the personal qualities of the leader, the leadership of a state inheres in roles and offices.   T

17. Assigning power by roles does not inherently create inequality.   F

18. Tyranny, the arbitrary or oppressive use of power, is an ever-present danger in all hierarchical organizations.   T

19. The pitfall of tyranny can usually be avoided by a balance of power among authoritative roles.   T

20. Cherokee peace chiefs and war chiefs are a good example of the dangers of tyranny in any hierarchical system.   T

21. The Polynesian and Melanesian systems of government were both based on the principle of power accruing to charismatic individuals.   F

22. Polynesian chiefs enjoyed the advantage of being able to rely on the support of their followers without constantly having to prove their personal abilities.   T

23. In many places, role-based power systems emerged as priesthoods.   T

24. In all cultures, there is some separation between religion and politics.   **F**

25. Chiefdoms are rarely theocratic.   **F**

26. Among the ancient Egyptians, state and religion were kept carefully separate.   **F**

27. Characteristics of the state include bureaucracy and the ability to back up authority with force.   **T**

28. The word bureaucracy means "desk power."   **T**

29. A bureaucracy is a systematic hierarchy of interlinked roles or offices marked by overt levels of authority and power.   **T**

30. Bureaucracies are only found in industrialized cultures.   **F**

31. The commoner-filled bureaucracy of the Bantu reflected the fact that no ruler could fully trust his clansmen.   **T**

32. Social traps common to bureaucracies include rigidity, incompetence, and conflicts between the individual interests of the bureaucrats and the needs of the state.   **T**

33. The basic idea that underlies the nation-state is the idea that the ethnic group is the natural unit of government.   **T**

34. In early Europe, the territory of the kingdom was just as important as the ethnicity of the subjects.   **F**

35. From a global perspective, the nation-state is both an attainable and desirable concept.   **F**

36. Most modern countries are nation-states organized around a single ethnic group.   **F**

37. The association of state with ethnic group is one of the great social traps of modern times.   **T**

38. All states were formed by expansion through conquest.   **F**

39. Some scholars claim that the state is a cultural mechanism by which cooperation can be achieved with non-kin.   **T**

40. The replacement of loyalty to the ethnic group with loyalty to the bureaucratic state is easily achieved.   **F**

41. According to most scholars since Machiavelli, force is not a necessary dimension of the state.   **F**

42. The Stalinist regime in the USSR demonstrated the benefits that accrue when an absolute ruler tries to remodel society in the absence of consensual legitimacy.   **F**

43. Taxation is a means for specialized governments to raise the funds necessary to carry out their work.   **T**

44. Taxation makes the government a collection point of wealth for redistribution.   **T**

45. Today the only institutions that command large amounts of money are governments and corporations.   **T**

46. There are other social institutions in the U.S. that can solve the problems of poverty, welfare, etc. besides the government.   **F**

47. Modern-day pressures are out of line with primate, foraging, horticultural and agricultural heritage.   **T**

Multiple Choice

1. Government:
   a. is any set of social processes for doing the basic political jobs
   b. is the same as the state
   c. becomes unwieldy when it must address social problems far removed from its core tasks
   d. does not exist in stateless societies
   e. all of the above
   * f.____ and ____ (a and c)

2. Statelss societies can be governed through:
   a. families
   b. ceremonial groups
   c. lineages
   d. charismatic and powerful individuals
   * e. all of the above
   f. all of the above except ____

3. Hopi society:
   a. is matrilineal and matrilocal
   b. is organized through totemic clans
   c. was among the first to institute tribal government
   d. does its basic governing jobs in the course of carrying out religious ceremony
   e. all of the above
   * f. all of the above except ____ (c)

4. Lineage systems:
   a. can be used politically to control warfare
   b. work to determine who fights with and against whom
   c. effectively perform the tasks of government
   d. provide for a permanent set of representatives of a given society vis-a-vis outsiders
   e. all of the above
   * f. all of the above except ____ (d)

5. Ramage:
   a. refers to the pattern formed by the branches of a tree
   b. opens the road toward state organization
   c. results from the introduction of inequality of lineages into a lineage structure
   d. depends on charismatic big men for its success as a political system
   e. all of the above
   * f. all of the above except ____ (d)

67

6. The Melanesian big man system:
   a. depends on the personal skills and charismatic leadership of individuals
   b. involves the subsistence strategy of the redistribution of goods
   c. contains the seeds of a social trap
   d. is one way of governing a stateless society
 * e. all of the above
   f. all of the above except _____

7. Stateless societies:
   a. rely on a hierarchical structure to solve problems
   b. always have little respect for nature
 * c. often believe that allowing power to inhere in permanent offices is dangerous and should be avoided
   d. do not encourage ceremonial organizations
   e. all of the above expect _____

8. Characteristics of the state include:
   a. hierarchy and social inequality
   b. roles marked by recognized offices with inherent power
   c. bureaucracy
   d. the ever-present danger of tyranny
 * e. all of the above
   f. all of above except _____

9. A good example of a balance of power in a society with centralized leadership can be found in:
   a. Hopi villages
   b. Melanesian big men
   c. Tiv lineages
 * d. Cherokee peace chiefs and war chiefs
   e. Navajo families
   f. all of the above

10. Polynesian chiefs:
   a. must, like the Melanesian big men, use their personal charisma and skill to gain their positions of leadership
   b. have to personally obligate their followers to support them
 * c. have inherited positions that followers are culturally obligated to support
   d. can support warfare, art, and the redistribution of goods, but on a much smaller scale than Melanesian big men
   e. all of the above except _____

11. Role-based power systems:
    a. exist only in secular political systems
    b. can take the form of priesthoods
    c. often combine religious and political leadership in the same authoritative roles
    d. exist only in societies that have developed the state
    e. all of the above except ____
  * f. ____ and ____ (b and c)

12. To say that chiefdoms are usually theocratic means that:
    a. the chief is largely responsible for the society's economy
    b. the chief must be responsible for the equitable redistribution of goods
    c. the chief assumes only political functions
  * d. submission to the chief's authority is like a religious congregation's submission to a priest
    e. all of the above
    f. ____ and ____

13. Chiefdoms are characterized by:
    a. centralized leadership
    b. redistribution of goods in the hands of the leaders
    c. force that backs up authority
    d. leadership based on hereditary status
    e. all of the above
  * f. all of the above except ____ (c)

14. A social trap in the ancient Egyptian system of leadership was:
    a. using force to back up authority
    b. integrating political and religious leadership
    c. distinguising precisely between priest and ruler
  * d. warring between competing rulers
    e. all of the above

15. The state:
    a. is a specialized institution that does the basic political jobs
    b. differs from chiefdoms in that it adds the use of force to back up its centralized authority
    c. differs from the big man system in that it adds the principle of role
    d. involves the development of a bureaucracy
  * e. all of the above
    f. all of the above except ____

16. Specific characteristics of bureaucracies include:
    a. systematic authority relations among recognized officials
    b. interlinked offices characterized by defined rights and duties
    c. strict separation between office and incumbent
    d. a hierarchical status system
  * e. all of the above
    f. all of the above except ____

17. Soga (Bantu) rulers turn to non-royal clans to build their bureaucracies because:
    a. there are genetic defects in the royal clans
    b. rulers can only marry the daughters of commoners
    c. they are known for their greater efficiency
  * d. they cannot compete with the ruler for the rulership
    e. all of the above
    f. none of the above

18. Social traps that may cause bureaucracies to fail include all of the following *except*:
    a. rigidity—the inability to adapt to change
    b. incompetence of the bureaucrats
  * c. the interlinking of the bureaucratic roles
    d. conflicts between the individual interests of the bureaucrats and the aims and tasks assigned to the bureaucracy

19. The idea of the nation-state:
    a. correlates the ethnic group with a specific territory
    b. reached its greatest philosophical development in the German romantic idea of the *Volk*
    c. was central to the peace process at the end of World War I
    d. often leads to tremendous resentment among ethnic groups not provided with their own nation-state
    e. completely separates ethnic loyalty from patriotism
  * f. all of the above except _____ (e)

20. Correlation of ethnic group with state in today's world would, in most cases:
    a. be a desirable and attainable goal
    b. involve minor difficulties that could be worked out easily
  * c. involve mass movement of peoples, loss of property and life, and unimaginable agonies of displacement of peoples and culture
    d. restore a Golden Age of peace and freedom to the planet
    e. be the next logical step in human evolution

21. Most countries today:
    a. are nation-states consisting of a single ethnic group
    b. include only two or at most three ethnic groups
  * c. are multi-ethnic and multicultural
    d. are on the brink of global war
    e. none of the above

22. Theories on the origin of the state hold that:
    a. states are formed as a result of the expansion of one people by the conquest of another
    b. the state emerged as a cultural mechanism by which cooperation can be achieved with non-kin
    c. the state formed as a social solution to problems created by population growth or by changes of ecological niche
    d. the state is a means of providing a coordinated labor supply for large-scale projects like irrigation
    * e. all of the above
    f. all of the above except _____

23. As states begin to develop through new levels of organization:
    a. earlier types of organization begin to disappear
    b. people stop dealing with kin and start to deal only with non-kin
    c. wider communities form, while the narrower ones are abandoned
    d. all of the above except _____
    * e. none of the above

24. A successful state is marked by the following characteristics that are not characteristic of other forms of government:
    a. its citizens are loyal to a bureaucracy
    b. its sovereignty is maintained through force, when authority fails
    c. it must maintain the consent of the governed
    d. its dissenters are imprisoned or dismissed from the system
    e. all of the above
    * f. all of the above except _____ (d)

25. Social problems such as welfare, social security, and unemployment insurance:
    a. can be solved by a variety of American institutions
    b. exemplify the rapid growth of the responsibilities and problems facing the contemporary state
    c. might possibly be better solved by other social institutions not yet invented
    d. all of the above
    * e. all of the above except _____ (a)

Essay

1. Discuss the relationship of government to the state. How are stateless societies governed? Give specific examples. Explain the advantages and the limitations of each governmental system you discuss.

2. Describe the Melanesian big man system. What makes it likely to become a social trap for the big men who succeed in that system?

3. Compare and contrast the Melanesian and Polynesian systems of government. What are the relative advantages and disadvantages of each?

4. Identify the social traps in:
   a) the Melanesian big man system
   b) Polynesian chiefdoms
   c) bureaucracies
   d) the idea of the nation-state

5. a. From simple government by family or individual in egalitarian societies, to complex government by specialized institution in hierarchical societies, trace the evolution of the state, using specific examples.

   b. Now consider: Is this a one-way process? Is the state always better? Evaluate each governmental form you discussed for its advantages and its social traps. Which governmental form would you prefer to head up? Why?

6. What do you think of the idea of the nation-state? What would happen if the idea of the nation-state were to become the guiding force in global politics? What will happen if it doesn't?

7. Has the U.S. been successful in earning the loyalty of its ethnic groups? Has the USSR? Why or why not?

8. a. Discuss the origins, characteristics, specific tasks, and special problems of the state.
   b. What do you envision as the future for the state?

9. Use what you have learned in this course to explain Bohannan's statement, "Modern-day pressures are out of line with our primate heritage, with our foraging heritage, and with our horticultural and agricultural heritage."

Born Equal?

9

What students should get out of the chapter . . .

Inequality of persons is based on a complex set of criteria that emerge from complex systems of division of labor, and from the quest for and maintenance of social power. People can be ranked by their social roles, by the groups into which they were born or which they choose, by the categorization of the work they do, or by cultural traits they manipulate.

Institutions of inequality are destructive when some persons are not allowed to develop their talents fully. The human species and human culture need all the talent available.

Films and Videos

North Indian Village. 32 min. color. 1959. University of California Extension Media Center. Study of the village of Khalapur between 1953 and 1955. Windowless mud houses and unpaved roads are still characteristic of the conditions found in many villages. Cultivation of the land is the principal means of livelihood. Contaminated water, primitive cooking on earthen floors, and dirt and dung still create a major health problem. Caste system is illustrated. We also see typical preparations for a village marriage.

Chapter 9

Test Items

True/False

1. Inequality is a basic feature of all complex societies.   **T**

2. The term social stratification refers to pariah institutions.   **F**

3. Pariahs in most cultures are recognized for their high social status.   **F**

4. The caste situation in the U.S. and India is much the same.   **F**

5. Human schemata are reflections of the natural order.   **F**

6. Institutions of rank arise when people are categorized and those categories are then arranged hierarchically.   **T**

7. Sometimes social scientists confuse ranking systems in the U.S. or Europe with ranking systems in other societies.   **T**

8. Many societies have ranking systems very similar to those of Europe and the U.S.   **F**

9. The schemata of some societies define some people out of social existence.   **T**

10. A caste in pre-independence India was a corporate group composed of extended families.   **T**

11. Pre-independence castes in India were mostly exogamous.   **F**

12. All the members of a given caste have to work at the occupation traditionally assigned to that caste.   **F**

13. The Indian caste system was legally abolished soon after India's independence.   **T**

14. Social mobility of individuals within the caste system was easily available through intermarriage and occupational skill.   **F**

15. Social mobility within the caste system was impossible.   **F**

16. Contemporary European ideas about ranking of people and groups no longer have anything to do with the feudal estate system.   **F**

17. Medieval yeomen owed armed service and a percentage of their agricultural production to their feudal lord, but received nothing in return.   **F**

18. Medieval serfs are a good example of a European caste.   **F**

19. Medieval serfs were in much the same position as nineteenth century American slaves.   **F**

20. Medieval estates are structured and organized groups, while Indian castes are simply categories of people.   **F**

21. In India, family and class interests were always the same, while in the U.S., these interests often clash.   **T**

22. Anthropologist Lloyd Warner codified the American class system in the 1940s.   **T**

23. In the American class system, rank is determined by prestige and occupation.   **T**

24. It has been learned that, in the U.S., sexual behavior and voting behavior vary with social class.   **T**

25. From an anthropological viewpoint the American class system is a system of ranked culture traits.   **T**

26. Generally speaking, in India, culture was ascribed; in the U.S., it is selected and achieved.   **T**

27. Slave systems have little in common with caste and class systems.   **T**

28. Slavery exists when one person is under contractual obligation to another.   **F**

29. In the modern West, all our legal rights derive from the principles of kinship, citizenship, or contract.   **T**

30. Slaves were common in hunting-gathering societies.   **F**

31. Forty-three percent of societies that used advanced agriculture institutionalized slavery.   **T**

32. The great majority of pastoral societies were slavery-free.   **F**

33. Most major advanced civilizations passed through a period of slavery.   **T**

34. Slavery was a recognized institution by the time written records start.   **T**

35. Slaves among the ancient Greeks were segregated and were treated like social pariahs.   **F**

36. All slavery systems are marked by the values of the social system of which they are a part.   **T**

37. The primary source of slaves in most societies was purchase from other groups or from slave traders.   **F**

38. In much of traditional Africa, the kinship group could agree to turn a man into a non-kinsman through the performance of a simple ritual.   **T**

39. Slaves could be captured, purchased, or born into their positions.   **T**

40. Some slaves in various societies enjoyed wealth, power, and very high status.   **T**

41. Slavery hardly existed at all in Africa until the European slave traders got involved.   **F**

42. A human pawn is another form of slave.   **F**

43. In some places, whole social groups are servile to other groups.   **T**

44. Pariahs are outsiders without being foreigners.   **T**

45. The economic activities of pariah groups are irrelevant to the functioning of their society.   **F**

46. Slaves are pariahs.   **F**

47. Race, ethnicity, and gender may all lead to cultural distinctions that create a basis for the assignment of inequality.   **T**

48. Genetic physical differences between races necessarily result in social problems.   **F**

49. Geographically isolated human groups may begin to diverge in physical type from other isolated groups.   **T**

50. The assignment of race is based on scientific systems of genetic classification.   **F**

51. Updated Western techniques of genetic research now insure that the study of race will soon provide a good basis for developing a comprehensive science of humankind.   **F**

52. Racism was a major social problem in ancient Greece and Rome.   **F**

53. The primary criterion for hatred of one group by another in the European Middle Ages was racism.   **F**

54. Native Americans were never enslaved on a large scale by the colonists because, once enslaved, they quickly died.   T

55. The first Africans to be brought to the North American colonies were brought as indentured servants.   T

56. Darwin worked to add the idea of the survival of the fittest to racist doctrine.   F

57. According to anthropologist Ruth Benedict, understanding race persecution requires an investigation not of race, but of persecution.   T

58. After blacks were emancipated at the end of the Civil War, there was no social category to fit them into and they drifted into pariah status.   T

59. The most widespread inequality in the modern world is that based on race.   F

60. The most widespread inequality in the modern world is that based on gender.   T

61. Both ethnicity and race are ascribed on the basis of birth.   T

62. Ethnics are always organized into formal social groups.   F

63. In the United States, ethnic culture is constantly created anew in response to new contexts.   T

64. Ethnicity and class are interchangeable categories.   F

65. The American ethnic system, like those of most other peoples, holds that if anybody is ethnic, everybody is, and so defines all citizens in terms of an ethnic group.   F

66. Bohannan believes that it will eventually be possible to create a society free of institutions of rank.   F

67. Bohannan says that one of the worst results of social inequality is that many individuals are prevented from fully developing their talents.   T

Multiple Choice

1. Inequalities appear in societies where:
   * a. division of labor is highly specialized
   b. economic organization is simplified
   c. bureaucracies are not part of the government system
   d. roles and culture traits are rarely officially ranked
   e. none of the above

2. Distinctions for imposing inequality can be made on the basis of:
   a. occupation and wealth
   b. rank of the parents
   c. race, ethnicity, and gender
   d. education
   * e. all of the above
   f. all of the above except _____

3. Human schemata are:
    a. ethnocentric and provincial
    b. reflections of the natural order
    c. cultural shortcuts for thinking and acting
    d. expressions of cultural values
    e. all of the above
  * f. all of the above except _____ (b)

4. Traps some social scientists fall into when they think about rank usually do *not* include:
    a. confusing the ranking systems of other cultures with those of one's own culture
    b. too-literal adherence to specific ideological doctrines about ranking
    c. discriminating against the people in the pariah categories of other cultures
    d. encouraging endogamy in the caste and estate systems
  * e. _____ and _____ (c and d)
    f. any of the above

5. A caste in pre-independence India:
    a. was a corporate group composed of extended families
    b. had a generally understood organizational structure
    c. had diffuse and easily permeable boundaries
    d. was mostly exogamous
  * e. all of the above except _____ and _____ (c and d)

6. From a Western point of view, the most important characteristic of the caste system is its:
    a. social inequality
    b. linking of certain groups with certain occupations
    c. institutionalization of poverty
  * d. lack of opportunity for social mobility
    e. all of the above

7. The three primary estates in the estate system of medieval Europe included:
    a. castles, manors, and huts
    b. landowners, yeomanry, and merchants
    c. nobles, princes, and commoners
  * d. nobility, serfs, and yeomanry
    e. none of the above

8. Which sentence identifies the major differences between the medieval European estate and the pre-independence Indian caste?
  * a. A caste is a structured and organized group, while an estate is a category of people.
    b. An estate is a structured and organized group, while a caste is a category of people.
    c. A caste is a system of social stratification, while an estate is marked by religious function and practice.
    d. While estates classify people on the basis of achieved status, castes classify them on the basis of ascribed status.
    e. None of the above.

78

9. Which sentence is not true?
   a. Americans see the lack of a kinship base for ranking as a positive opportunity for social mobility.
   b. In the U.S., family and class interests often clash.
   * c. In the U.S., family and class interests are one and the same.
   d. In the American class system, the primary criterion for rank is material culture.
   e. Before 1925, some people thought that American society was not stratified.
   f. Before 1925, social scientists were little interested in the American system of stratification.

10. American anthropologist Lloyd Warner:
    a. held that American society did not have a class system
    b. wrote important studies of the medieval European estate system and the Indian caste system
    * c. codified the American class system
    d. said that the lower class was composed of the poverty-stricken and the chronically unemployable
    e. all of the above except ____

11. The immediate post-World War II period was probably:
    a. normal for the U.S.
    b. a sign of our cultural deterioration
    * c. an unusual time of great opportunity
    d. served as a model for equal opportunity for blacks
    e. all of the above
    f. all of the above except ____ and ____

12. The American class system:
    a. is a system of ranked culture traits that are not irrevocably ascribed but can be achieved
    b. is an illusion, because there is no American culture
    c. is malleable
    d. influences the sexual behavior, voting behavior, and religious behavior of its members
    e. all of the above
    * f. all of the above except ____ (b)

13. If Americans want to change social classes, the first thing they must do is:
    a. move to another country
    * b. learn the culture of the group they are moving into
    c. acquire wealth
    d. marry someone from the group they want to join
    e. change communities

14. Systems of slavery:
    a. have much in common with class and caste systems
    b. involve rights in people derived from kinship, citizenship, and/or contractual obligation
    c. give slaves contractual and kinship rights in their masters
    d. are rare among the major advanced civilizations
    e. all of the above
    * f. none of the above

15. Slaves in ancient Greece:
    a. were often manumitted on an individual basis
    b. performed most of the activities of full-fledged citizens
    c. occasionally held political office
    d. did not usually gain financial profit from their work
    e. all of the above
 * f. all of the above except _____ (c)

16. In various societies at various times, slaves have been obtained through:
    a. purchase from kin or community
    b. capture
    c. the selling of children
    d. birth
 * e. all of the above
    f. all of the above except _____

17. According to Bohannan, children could be purchased to provide infertile families with heirs in:
    a. India
    b. Native America
    c. Sri Lanka
 * d. China
    e. Greenland

18. Their lack of legal rights and their resultant total dependence on their masters often meant that slaves:
    a. were readily brought into the kinship systems of their masters and considered kin
    b. could change masters fairly easily
    c. could never be freed
 * d. were often considered more trustworthy by their masters than contractual partners and employees
    e. none of the above

19. Slavery everywhere reflects:
    a. history's caprice
    b. the tendency of *homo sapiens* to be aggressive and inhumane
    c. caste and class
 * d. the values and social structure of the culture in which it exists
    e. all of the above except _____
    f. all of the above

20. Most American ideas about slavery are derived from:
    a. the slavery systems of ancient Greece and Rome
    b. the buying and selling of children in China
    c. the samurai system of Japan
 * d. the forcible transportation of Africans to the Americas
    e. all of the above except _____

21. When one whole social group is specifically servile to one other social group, anthropologists call this a system of:
    a. servitude
    b. patronage
  * c. clientage
    d. pawning
    e. slavery

22. Pariah:
    a. is an Indian word for an unowned scavenger dog
    b. is not part of the accepted rank system
    c. means someone who is an outsider without being a foreigner
    d. indicates someone who is both socially and economically irrelevant to the culture
    e. all of the above
  * f. all of the above except _____ (d)

23. Social evaluations used as a basis for inequality include differences in:
    a. physical type
    b. jobs assigned according to gender
    c. ethnic cultures
    d. wealth
    e. speech and mannerisms
  * f. all of the above

24. A major mistake made by the founders of the field of physical anthropology was:
  * a. the premise that in the beginning there were "pure" races
    b. the discovery that some geographically isolated human groups began to divulge in physical type from other human groups
    c. the belief that early humans engaged in far-flung migrations
    d. the notion of the specialization of isolated gene pools
    e. none of the above

25. Today, the important question in the field of research into the genetic bases of race is:
    a. Do races exist?
    b. Are the members of some races less intelligent than the members of some other races?
    c. Are the members of some races more physically fit than the members of other races?
    d. What criteria should be used to distinguish one race from another?
  * e. What problem is the classification of races designed to solve?
    f. None of the above.

26. Race:
    a. is a cultural classification designed to deal with social problems
    b. is a scientific classification based on definable genetic differences
    c. like ethnicity, can be a useful tag for social identification
    d. does not provide the basis for a science of humankind
    e. all of the above
  * f. all of the above except _____ (b)

27. Charles Darwin:
    a. associated racism with nationalism
    b. added the idea of the survival of the fittest to racist doctrine
    c. perfected techniques for measuring people's skulls to determine their race
  * d. insisted that survival of the fittest had only to do with adaptation to a given environment, and had nothing to do with racist doctrine
    e. all of the above except _____

28. The most widespread inequality in the modern world is that based on:
    a. race
    b. ethnicity
    c. socioeconomic status
    d. physical disability
  * e. gender

29. Ethnicity:
    a. is about distinctions made on the basis of culture
    b. is usually ascribed on the basis of birth
    c. gives individuals a sense of cultural distinctiveness
    d. requires contrast with at least one other ethnic category
    e. is created and recreated in response to changing circumstances
  * f. all of the above

30. According to Bohannan, the American ethnic system:
    a. is like the ethnic systems of other countries that assign an ethnic identity to everyone
    b. is irrational in that it claims that some citizens belong to ethnic groups while others do not
    c. hyphenates some Americans and not others
    d. allows many Americans to maintain what they see as their cultural identities and works to make American society safe for differences
    e. all of the above
  * f. all of the above except _____ (a)

31. According to Bohannan, it is probably not possible to:
    a. create a society free of institutions of servitude
  * b. create a society free of institutions of rank
    c. separate the idea of a person's work from the socially ascribed identity of the person, especially for women
    d. eliminate slavery, pariahism, and poverty
    e. equalize the cultural valuations of women and men

32. Which of the following is not one of the four advantages that high rank bestows (the four Ps):
    a. power
    b. property
  * c. privacy
    d. pleasure
    e. prestige

33. According to Bohannan, the worst thing about inequality is that it:
* a. prevents many individuals from fully developing their talents
   b. insures systems of hierarchy and rank in all societies
   c. perpetuates ethnocentrism
   d. encourages people in power to seek more power
   e. all of the above

Essay

1. Name some of the bases for determining inequality utilized by various societies. Provide specific examples of each.

2. Describe the Indian caste system. What makes each caste a "subculture" as opposed to a mere agglomeration of people?

3. Explain the difference between the medieval estate system of Western Europe and the *jati* system of India. Why are these two systems often confused?

4. Describe slavery in its various forms. What have been slavery's roles in most major civilizations?

5. What is a pawn? What do pawns have in common with indentured servants? How do these two differ?

6. Describe at least three institutions of servitude that have functioned across cultures. On what basis is servitude assigned? How do the various servile groups you describe fit into the larger society of which they are a part? What common patterns emerge?

7. Why did anthropologist Ruth Benedict compare Nazi race policy to the Spanish Inquisition's policy on religion? What point was she trying to make?

8. Discuss the similarities and differences you can see in the cultural status of the Untouchables in India and American blacks before and after slavery.

9. What is a pariah? a pariah group? Name at least five groups that you can think of that have at one time or another been culturally assigned pariah status. What (besides pariah status) do these groups have in common?

10. Evaluate race as a scientific and social concept. What does race have to do with human evolution? How useful is the concept of race? What is it good for? What harm does it do?

11. Consider American ethnicity. List as many American ethnic groups as you can think of. Are these organized social groups? Why do they exist? What is odd about American ethnic classifications as compared to those of most other countries.

12. What does gender inequality in the U.S. have to do with family violence?

13. Consider gender inequality in the U.S. today.
   a. What forms does it take? Describe your personal experiences with gender inequality.
   b. Based on both your personal experiences and your knowledge about American society, evaluate our cultural status in relation to the ultimate goal of gender equality. Do you think we will achieve it? If so, when? What do we stand to gain? to lose?

14. Where do you personally stand in relation to the four Ps? Do you want them? Which ones? Why? What will you try to do to get the ones you want? What will it mean if you achieve them? If you don't?

15. What, according to Bohannan, is the most damaging feature of social inequality? Why do you think he feels this way? Who pays the price for this type of damage?

16. Must racism, genderism, ethnocentrism and nationalism always be a part of human societies? Why or why not? What about servitude? rank? Do you think we can all ever be truly equal? Explain.

CUMULATIVE ESSAY QUESTIONS

1. What type of government are hunter-gatherers most likely to have? horticulturalists? agriculturalists? pastoralists? industrialists? In other words, using specific examples, correlate government type with subsistence method.

2. Pick four disparate societies, and discuss them in comparative fashion in terms of subsistence method, government type, economic system, and systems for conflict resolution and the maintenance of social order. Then evaluate their relative success at avoiding social traps.

3. What do you think is the most adaptive subsistence strategy so far invented by humans? Why? The most adaptive economic strategy? Why? Are these two from the same type of society? What does that suggest for the future of humanity?

4. Evaluate the effects of each subsistence method, government type, and economic system on the social ranking of people. What can you conclude about the possibilities for all people to be equal?

5. Consider economy and government. How do the economic principles of reciprocity, redistribution, and the market correlate with governmental types (families, ceremonial groups, lineages, ramages, big men, chiefdoms, bureaucracies, states)? Could a state base its economy on reciprocity? Could a tribe of hunter-gatherers base their economy on redistribution or the market principle? Why or why not?

6. Consider the possibility of a world government for the people of the Planet Earth.
   a. Where would the seat of government be located? Under what governmental principles (unicentric, bicentric, multicentric) would a world government best operate? What would be its constituent units (countries? nation-states? ethnic groups? races? religious groups? regions? continents?)? Why?
   b. How would such a government gain the loyalty of its citizens? preserve harmony and order? How would it resolve disputes between its constituent parts? Compared to the present world situation, what would be the potential advantages of such a government? the potential disadvantages?
   c. Under what cultural and economic conditions might such a government be created? Do you think it should be?

Symbols
Language and Art

10

What students should get out of the chapter . . .

In animal behavior, the realm of meaning is usually limited to signs—generally (there are some simple exceptions) it lacks the use of symbols. Although human meaning involves the brain and receptors, it is largely symbolic and hence purely cultural. Languages (including the gestures that accompany them) and art are the two most common media for expressing meaning.

Films and Videos

Art

Discovering the Moche. 25 min. color. 1979. University of California Extension Media Center. An introduction to the art and culture of the Moche, who flourished between 100 B.C. and A.D. 700 in the arid river valleys of Peru's northern coastal plain. Shows how the study of Moche art, in conjunction with archaeological evidence, ethnographical analogy to present-day Peruvian Indians, and careful reading of early Spanish accounts, can be employed to reconstruct this ancient culture and interpret it in its own terms. Explains how to understand Moche art, and how art served as a means of communication in Moche life.

Gripping Beast. 15 min. color. Year unknown. Audience Planners. An animated film made in Denmark tracing the development of the Viking "Gripping Beast" art motif from its naturalistic beginnings to its late, highly-schematic form.

Imaginero. 52 min. color. 1971. University of California Extension Media Center. Classic ethnographic portrait of a deeply spiritual religious image-maker living on the high Argentine plateau. Locally revered for his cactus-wood crucifixes, miniature shrines, religious paintings, and church decorations, he sees both his art and his life not as self-expression but rather as a means of honoring God, Christ, and the Virgin Mary.

Matjemosh. 27 min. color. 1964. University of California Extension Media Center. Matjemosh is a woodcarver of the Asmat tribe in New Guinea. This ethnological documentary shows him using a stone hammer and iron chisel to carve wooden figures and decorate bamboo signal horns of the kind his ancestors used to blow on headhunting raids. He makes a drum out of a log, hollowing the inside into the traditional conical shape and polishing the outside with a shell.

Mbira: The Technique of the Mbira dza Vadzimu. 19 min. color. 1976. Penn State Audio-Visual Services. Examines in detail the use of the traditional African mbira in the cultural life of the Mashona people of Rhodesia. Introduces the musical technique and sound of the mbira dza vadzimu, played by Ephrat Mujuru, a leading mbira player. Using animation and freeze-frame techniques, the film includes a demonstration of some of the rhythmic and harmonic elements of the music, of the use of improvisation, of different styles of playing a song, and of the combination of two mbiras in a duet.

The Path. 34 min. color. 1972. University of California Extension Media Center. Records an entire tea ceremony, a traditional Japanese art form that is often identified as a microcosm of traditional Japanese culture. The film's style reflects, as does the ceremony itself, the deeper meaning of formal Japanese art, and requires the viewer to confront, with a minimum of narration, the perceptual framework of Japanese aesthetics in practice. Beautifully understated cinematography captures the meaning and, especially, the feeling of the ceremony.

Language

Invisible Walls. 12 min. black and white. 1969. University of California Extension Media Center. Focuses on common American beliefs about personal space, showing that people encase themselves in invisible walls about eighteen inches from their bodies and that violation of these imaginary walls causes a feeling of discomfort. An actor and actress are shown randomly stopping unsuspecting subjects in Los Angeles shopping centers while hidden cameras record the results. Analysis reveals several patterns of subject response that seem to be culturally derived.

Chapter 10

Test Items

True/False

1. Speech is the same as language.   F

2. Apes have the intelligence to use language.   T

3. Apes cannot communicate with human symbols.   F

4. Humans are the only primates who communicate through the use of spoken language.   T

5. The meanings of symbols are arbitrary.   T

6. A sign is anything that allows a person or animal to infer the existence of something else.   T

7. Symbols allow humans to add agreed-upon meaning to signs.   T

8. Humans have an innate, genetically-based capacity for learning language.   T

9. Learning language has to do with catching on to the idea of symbols.   T

10. Helen Keller's experience teaches us that the principle of symbolization is basic to human communication.   T

11. Language is a human symbol system.   T

12. Some languages are primitive and unable to change in response to changing circumstances.   F

13. Most gestures mean the same thing across cultures   F

14. A symbol can mean only one thing at a time.   F

15. One major purpose of ethnographic analysis is to understand the symbols of the culture being studied.   T

16. Explanation lies at the foundation of every culture.   T

17. Linguistics is the study of the evolution of the human vocal apparatus.   F

18. Of the myriad sounds that humans can produce, only a small number are used to build any language.   T

19. The English language uses about seventy-five sounds.   F

20. A phoneme is a minimal unit of meaning.   F

21. The same phonemes are utilized in all human languages.   F

22. A morpheme is a minimal unit of sound.   F

23. Syntax means the way the phonemes and morphemes of a given language are organized and arranged to make sense.   T

24. Cultural anthropologists often come up with basic units of culture as simple and straightforward as phonemes and morphemes.   F

25. The human brain has a genetic capacity to generate words and grammar from a few rules.   T

26. Saying "runned" instead of "ran" shows that children can't follow the rules of grammar.   F

27. Language establishes a perceptual screen between the natural world and any human experience of it.   T

28. According to Edward Sapir, any number of languages can represent the same social reality.   F

29. Benjamin Lee Whorf claimed that language directly influences the way people perceive reality.   T

30. According to Bohannan, the purpose of art is to communicate ideas and emotions.   T

31. Doodles are culture-free expressions of the individual psyche.   F

32. Decorations are used across cultures to enhance the stimulus value of what is decorated.   T

33. Cross-cultural methods of body decoration include clothing, jewelry, paint, cosmetics, tattooing, and scarification.   T

34. All decoration has a specific, decodable meaning.   F

35. According to Bohannan, any object with a message can be considered art.   F

36. The affecting presence of a piece of art means that it arouses emotion.   T

37. Art is recognized as a special realm in all human cultures.   F

38. Every known human culture has a word for music.   F

39. Every known human culture has music.   T

40. Art is a unique combination of symbols, play and form.   F

41. While the essence of science is to dissect complexity into parts, the essence of art is to amalgamate many meanings into one complex symbol.   T

42. Anthropologists apply the scientific method to the cross-cultural understanding of art.   T

43. Play involves taking ideas out of their original context and using them in some other context.   T

44. The scientific investigation of play has led to the insight that children's play has little to do with the adult world.   F

45. Anthropologist Gregory Bateson was unable to find animal behavior that indicates unquestionably that the animals were aware they were engaging in play behavior.   F

46. Play is an essential part of art and learning.   T

47. Most individual artists are quite conscious of their own aesthetic.   F

48. All cultures have an overt and explicit artistic aesthetic.   F

49. Viewers of art in American culture generally perceive art indirectly, through the perceptual screen of their own preconceptions and the dictates of the experts.   T

50. Art works to rearrange perception of the material and social worlds.   T

Multiple Choice

1. Languages are:
   a. universal
   b. parochial
   c. the major vehicle for the culturization of communication
   d. shared by the members of a given cultural group
   e. human symbol systems
   * f. all of the above except _____ (a)

2. Human beings are the only primates who can:
   a. understand language
   b. use symbols
   c. use computers
   * d. communicate through spoken language
   e. all of the above
   f. all of the above except _____

3. A basic and essential step in learning language is:
   * a. grasping the principle of symbolization
   b. reading about the life of Helen Keller
   c. connecting with culture
   d. using words to communicate sensations
   e. learning a second language

4. Symbols can be:
   a. icons
   b. words
   c. paintings
   d. trees
   * e. all of the above
   f. all of the above except _____

5. The meanings of symbols:
   a. are intrinsic to the symbol
   b. are inherent in nature
   * c. are arbitrary and culturally assigned
   d. are universal across cultures
   e. all of the above
   f. all of the above except _____

6. Languages:
   a. change to accommodate changing circumstances
   b. are difficult for adults to learn
   c. are primitive when they are created by groups of primitive people
   d. usually have whatever words and grammar the people who speak them need to discuss and use their culture
   e. all of the above
   * f. all of the above except _____ (c)

91

7. Gestures:
    * a. are culturally specific sets of symbols that must be learned
    b. reflect inborn and innate genetic characteristics of humans
    c. are the same everywhere
    d. are the same for all speakers of one language
    e. all of the above except ____

8. Symbols are powerful because they:
    a. can communicate many meanings at once
    b. prevent us from being aware of connecting the meanings they communicate
    c. obscure complexity by making it seem simple
    d. link many different contexts together
    * e. all of the above

9. Which sentence is *not* true?
    a. Our perception of the physical universe comes to us through a symbolic screen of meaning.
    b. There are no primitive languages.
    c. Language strongly influences the way people perceive reality.
    d. People who speak or write well are often powerful because they can manipulate meaning.
    * e. Gestures are unimportant symbols in human communication.

10. Of the myriad sounds that humans can produce, most languages use:
    a. around 100
    b. fewer than 10
    * c. fewer than 50
    d. fewer than 500
    e. none of the above

11. A minimal unit of sound within a language is called:
    a. a morpheme
    b. an allomorph
    * c. a phoneme
    d. an allophone
    e. syntax

12. A morpheme is:
    a. a minimal unit of sound within a language
    b. a word
    c. anything that carries meaning
    * d. a minimal unit of meaning within a language
    e. a form of syntax
    f. a grammatical construct

13. The word "recycles" contains _____ morphemes:
    a. one
    b. two
  * c. three
    d. four
    e. five
    f. eight

14. Syntax:
    a. refers to the way phonemes and morphemes are strung together and organized
    b. has to do with using the elements of a given language to make sense
    c. encompasses grammar
    d. in many languages, involves tone and intonation
  * e. all of the above
    f. all of the above except _____

15. The fact that English-speaking children say "runned" instead of "ran" shows that:
    a. their linguistic skills are immature
  * b. they have internalized one of English's generative grammatical rules and can follow it
    c. they are not as intelligent as adults
    d. they do not yet understand the deep structure of the language
    e. all of the above
    f. all of the above except _____

16. Sapir's and Whorf's work suggests that:
    a. reality determines language
    b. all human minds work in basically the same way
    c. most people see the world in very similar ways
  * d. language influences people's perceptions of reality
    e. none of the above

17. People decorate themselves in order to:
    a. give themselves extra stimulus value
    b. send political messages
    c. convey sexual messages
    d. conform to commonly approved standards
    e. make themselves "glow"
  * f. all of the above

18. Art can be used to:
    a. sell things and propagandize
    b. enhance the stimulus value of an object
    c. add vitality to religion
    d. communicate the emotion and the intent of the artist
  * e. all of the above
    f. all of the above except _____

19. The process of the logical addition of elements to build up conceptualizations that lead to art proceeds in the following order:
    a. principles for judging good from bad, ritual representations, protection against witches, art as a special field
    b. doodling, magic, protection against witches, the affecting presence, art as a special field
    c. doodling, purposive decoration, the affecting presence, art as a special field, students of art
    d. doodling, decoration, dance, decorum
    * e. none of the above

20. Meaning in music may derive from:
    a. its incorporated words
    b. the context in which it is considered suitable
    c. the emotional affect that its sounds produce in hearers
    d. its value as a sign
    e. all of the above
    * f. all of the above except _____ (d)

21. Art is *not*:
    a. a complex web of symbols
    b. a kind of play
    c. a form of explanation
    d. a trigger for human thought and feeling
    e. a means of amalgamating many meanings into one whole
    * f. the dissection and systematic analysis of complexity

22. According to Bohannan, the scientific study of art:
    a. is a futile endeavor that ruins the ineffable quality of the art
    b. can produce understanding of the art that is as profound an experience as any produced by the art itself
    c. is fundamentally different from the artist's creation of the art
    d. involves the analysis of the art into its components
    e. all of the above
    * f. all of the above except _____ (a)

23. The recontexting quality of play Bohannan discusses means:
    a. that children can take rules and events from adult life and safely practice them in the world of make-believe
    b. taking a small slice of life and putting it into a special situation
    c. accepting the game as a rule-governed and bounded microcosmic reality
    d. that we can develop ideas from one context in a new context free of the burdens and limitations from which they stemmed
    * e. all of the above
    f. all of the above except _____

24. Play:
    a. is too fluid and evanescent to be scientifically investigated
  * b. changes the meaning of acts that would be taken seriously in other contexts
    c. is engaged in only by humans
    d. is engaged in more by female than by male primates
    e. has little to do with creativity and art
    f. all of the above

25. Which sentence is *not* true?
    a. Play is one of the best ways to learn culture.
    b. Any part of a given culture can be played with.
  * c. Play is an area of culturized behavior unrelated to serious art.
    d. Artists are sometimes considered dangerous because they dare to play with the most serious subjects.
    e. Play fosters artistic creativity.

26. Which sentence *is* true?
    a. Much of the value of art lies in the fact that it is most often experienced directly and cleanly by the viewer, without the interference of cultural screens and filters.
    b. Most artists are keenly aware of and very good at verbalizing their own aesthetic.
  * c. In industrial and postindustrial society, most viewers look at most art through a thick perceptual screen made up of cultural rules and aesthetics and the opinions of the experts.
    d. Simpler societies place as thick a perceptual screen between art and viewer as industrial societies do.
    e. Pornographic art that stirs the sexual appetites as well as the emotions should be classified in all cultures as trash.

Essay

1. What is the difference between a sign and a symbol? How does a symbol get its meaning? Why are symbols such powerful communicators?

2. Why do many Americans get very upset about flag-burning? What is a flag? Name one other very powerful symbol and discuss what happens when someone destroys or defaces it, and what such an act can mean.

3. What can Helen Keller's language-learning experience teach us about language and how we as humans learn it?

4. Discuss the relationship between language and ethnocentrism.

5. What is special about sharing symbols? Why?

6. Discuss the work of Edward Sapir and Benjamin Whorf in relation to the question: Does language shape reality, or does reality determine language?

7. What does Bohannan mean when he says that "language is power"?

8. Describe the essential qualities of art. What makes an object a work of art? How is that work of art different from an ordinary object?

9. For humans and primates, how is play different from the rest of life? What is its purpose? What benefits can play provide?

10. Consider the relationship between art and play. What do they have to do with each other? Use specific examples from your own cultural fund of knowledge to illustrate your points.

11. Why does Bohannan say that the recontexting quality of play is the essence of creativity? What does he mean? What does that have to do with art?

12. Discuss the relationship between culture and creativity, and evaluate the role of the individual artist in that relationship.

13. According to Bohannan, "art is any number of ways of rearranging perception of the material and social worlds so that new views of 'reality' can be tested and new appreciations of them projected." Think of at least two specific examples of art that do this. Describe these two, and evaluate their effectiveness.

Meaning
Creativity and Performance

11

What students should get out of the chapter . . .

Culture is performed and created by people—by each of us. Meanings are summarized in our performances and in our stories. Story and myth are to a people's worldview what theory is to science: the current best attempt at summing up meaning. Ritual reaffirms meanings by re-performance; ritual renews the commitment of both performers and audience to cultural values.

Films and Videos

Ajuba Dance and Drama Co. 20 min. color. 1979. University of Wisconsin Center for South Asian Studies. Introduces a troupe of popular entertainers in North India. Performing in private compounds, factory yards, and mango groves, they stage a type of theatre known as Nautanki, an amalgam of music, dance, comedy routines, and drama. The film allows viewers to see the performers in their everyday lives, meet the director, travel with his Ajuba troupe, watch them rehearse their lines and put on their makeup, and witness a performance itself.

A Balinese Trance Seance. 30 min. color. 1978. **Jero on Jero: A Balinese Trance Seance Observed.** 17 min. color. 1980. (Video contains both films.) Study guide available. Documentary Educational Resources. Jero Tapakan, a spirit medium in a small, central Balinese village, views herself in trance via an earlier videocassette recording provided by anthropologist Timothy Asch. Jero had a unique opportunity to spontaneously and consciously react to and reflect upon the experience of possession. Her comments provide insights into how she feels while possessed, her understanding of sorcery, and her humility in the presence of the supernatural world.

Eduardo the Healer. 55 min. color. 1978. Penn State Audio-Visual Services. Vivid documentary portrait of Eduardo Calderon, a fisherman, sculptor, and village shaman in Peru. Like Casteneda's Don Juan, he uses incantations, insightful psychological analysis, and hallucinogenic drugs to practice his healing arts. Includes a powerful nighttime sequence showing him curing a young man suffering from severe depression. Combines ethnographic veracity with beautiful cinematography and a fascinating life story.

Fixin' to Tell About Jack. 25 min. color. 1974. University of Illinois Film and Video Center. Ray Hicks, a mountain farmer of Beech Mountain, North Carolina, has a genius for telling traditional folktales, or "Jack Tales," each with specific details and histories that have been passed on from generation to generation. In this film, he tells the tales to a group of children. Illustrated by scenes of people working in the fields, wandering through the woods, and doing farm and household chores.

Floating in the Air, Followed by the Wind. 30 min. color. 1974. Indiana University Audio-Visual Center. Documents an annual Hindu religious festival at a pilgrimage center near Kuala Lumpur, Malaysia, in which some worshippers, led by a skilled guru, go into trance and pierce themselves with long needles and hooks without experiencing pain. Uses many direct statements by the penitents themselves to describe their beliefs and feelings.

Intrepid Shadows. 18 min. black and white silent. 1966. Museum of Modern Art. One of the most complex films and least understood by other Navajos, this film has been called by Margaret Mead "one of the finest examples of animism shown on film." Unlike the other films in the Navajos Film Themselves Series, this one deals with subjective rather than objective aspects of Navajo life. In the film, Al Clah attempts to reconcile the Western notion of God with his traditional Navajo notion of gods.

N/um Tchai. 25 min. black and white. 1966. Study guide available. Documentary Educational Resources. Documents a formalized Bushman curing ceremony in the Kalahari Desert. Shows an all-night "medicine dance" in which a number of men go into trance and exercise special curing powers. Divided into two parts: the first reviews typical dance scenes and explains their meaning, the second shows the ceremony without subtitles or narration. Shot in 1957 by John Marshall as part of the Peabody Expedition.

Salamanders: A Night at the Phi Delt House. 13 min. black and white. 1982. University of California Extension Media Center. For more than twenty years, fraternity members and their female guests at a major state university have celebrated the end of the school year by capturing and eating live salamanders. Fad or tradition? Rite of passage or inhumane and senseless act? This intriguing cinema-verite production documents the ritual and permits viewers to decide for themselves.

El Sebou': Egyptian Birth Ritual. 27 min. color. 1986. El Nil Research. Documents the Egyptian initiation of newborns on their seventh day of life. The ritual includes a journey to the old bazaar in Cairo and the pottery village in Fustat to purchase herbs and spices. During this rite-de-passage, newborns go through three universal phases crossing the threshold out of gender and status neutrality. The ritual links Egyptian birth to gender symbolism, traditional crafts, folk beliefs, strong womanhood, and the importance of family.

Chapter 11

Test Items

True/False

1. Creativity involves the abilities to question standard beliefs, values, and behaviors, and to recontext ideas.   T

2. Changing a culture from within requires the ability to question its basic ideas and assumptions.   T

3. Early anthropologists discovered that the people they called savages were highly creative and that their cultures changed rapidly.   F

4. Culture can be seen as a constantly evolving mixture of tools and meanings.   T

5. According to Bohannan, the history of human culture is the history of human creativity in response to challenges from the physical and cultural environments.   T

6. Anthropologists see no significant parallels between theatrical performances and everyday social life.   F

7. Children growing up in a given culture are often presented with unwritten ''scripts'' for the proper performance of cultural roles.   T

8. The performance of social roles is a scholarly concept that is generally irrelevant to most anthropological studies.   F

9. Individual role performances can never change the cultural script.   F

10. Recontexting is a creative social process of duplicating meanings from one cultural context to another.   T

11. Stories offer rich opportunities for recontexting many aspects of culture.   T

12. Folktales account for the origins of the world, while myths trace the adventures of heroes who have overcome obstacles.   F

13. Proverbs, riddles, and maxims are summaries of cultural lore.   T

14. Legends deal primarily with future events.   F

15. The humor in jokes often arises from the juxtaposition of ideas not usually associated in a given culture.   T

16. Most folklorists claim that anything that is mass produced can be considered folklore.   F

17. The Tiv interpret their own folktale about the vulva as degrading and insulting to women, since it clearly makes them into sex objects.   F

18. ''Road ghost'' stories are simply scary stories with no particular purpose except to frighten and thrill.   F

19. The Mexican-American story about the weeping woman can be interpreted as reinforcing a number of norms about proper social behavior.   T

20. Proverbs can serve to minimize deviation from culturally accepted norms.   T

21. Jokes are a powerful means of maintaining social control and punishing wrongdoers.   T

22. The only way that a nonliterate people can preserve and use their myths is by telling and performing them. **T**

23. Most people in most cultures consciously analyze their most important myths, and are aware of the pervasive influence of these myths on their everyday perceptions. **F**

24. Most anthropologists would say that the story of creation as written down in *Genesis* is true, while the Tiv story of the creation of the world by Aondo is false. **F**

25. What is important about myths from an anthropological perspective is not whether they are factually true or false but what they reveal about the core ideas of that culture and its premises for interpreting the world. **T**

26. People often think and feel through the medium of the complexity of their myths. **T**

27. The Dayak creation myth expresses the premise that everything contains its opposite. **T**

28. The creation myths of the Aranda of Australia express the deeply held view that there is no relationship between humans, the past, and the natural world. **F**

29. Ritual can be understood as the renewal of myth. **T**

30. Rites of passage do no more than mark biological transitions. **F**

31. The Ndembu Isoma ritual gives meaning to infertility while at the same time symbolically restoring fertility. **T**

32. During the boys' circumcision ceremony, the adoption by an older Gisu woman of the position taken for childbirth draws a strong symbolic parallel between childbirth and the ritual transition of boy to man created by circumcision. **T**

33. There are no rituals in American culture. **F**

Multiple Choice

1. Culture:
    a. is the product of human creativity
    b. gets changed by people when they get uncomfortable
    c. gets changed in response to environmental changes
    d. gets changed in response to new ideas within the culture
  * e. all of the above
    f. all of the above except _____

2. Creativity:
    a. is the primary mode by which humans adapt to the environment
    b. is prized for itself in some societies
    c. involves daring to question the standardized blueprint that a given culture provides for doing things
    d. involves recontexting ideas
  * e. all of the above
    f. all of the above except _____

3. Savages:
    a. could not be creative because their technology was too simple
    b. were primitive creatures who had fallen from God's grace
    c. were so weighed down by custom that they never changed anything in their cultures
    d. were slaves to superstition and taboo
    e. all of the above
  * f. none of the above

4. Bohannan's rule of cultural change and growth states that:
    a. even when people are getting the results they want, they keep tinkering with the system
    b. most cultures do not change
  * c. if humans find their ways of doing things inadequate, they search for better ways to do them
    d. humans are too baked in the cake of custom to break out of their cultural mold

5. Which sentence is true?
  * a. Once culture is created, constant performance keeps it alive.
    b. When culture ceases to be performed, it remains just as vital in the hearts and minds of its bearers.
    c. "Doing culture" often has nothing to do with performance.
    d. All the world's a stage, and all the men and women merely players.
    e. All of the above.
    f. All of the above except _____

6. The analogy of real life to drama:
    a. elaborated the notions of "actors" playing social "roles"
    b. helps anthropologists see that growing up and learning culture involves learning to play certain parts that are culturally scripted
    c. facilitates our understanding of human behavior and human interrelationships
  * d. all of the above
    e. all of the above except _____

7. Recontexting:
    a. is a creative social process of duplicating meanings from one cultural context to another
    b. almost always enforces reconsideration of the old meaning
    c. fosters creativity
    d. is impossible in the case of myth and ritual, which must be confined to the spiritual and religious realms
    e. all of the above
  * f. all of the above except _____ (d)

101

8. Stories:
   a. encapsulate culture
   b. must be told—not written
   c. allow the members of a culture to think many thoughts that would be unthinkable in the realm of real life
   d. allow effective examination and questioning of the basic premises of a culture
   e. all of the above
   * f. all of the above except ____(b)

9. Areas of culture in which stories and storytelling play essential roles include:
   a. history and biography
   b. religion
   c. theater and the visual arts
   d. education
   e. politics and business
   *f. all of the above

10. From a cross-cultural perspective, the most important forms of stories include:
   a. tales and legends
   b. jokes and riddles
   c. myths
   d. speeches
   e. all of the above
   * f. all of the above except ____(d)

11. Folktales:
   a. are generally nonreligious, nonhistorical stories that play with elemental themes and tensions
   b. often end with a moral that expresses a cultural value
   c. are purely entertaining
   d. are most effective when performed
   * e. all of the above except ____ (c)

12. The Tiv folktale about the vulva:
   a. devalues and degrades women by making them into sexual objects
   b. shows that men are the same the whole world over
   c. is interpreted by Tiv women as a reaffirmation that they have to be considered as people important in themselves
   d. is interpreted by the men to mean that they must be responsive to the needs of women
   e. all of the above
   * f. ____ and ____ (c and d)

102

13. Tiv stories and dances about diseases:
    a. show their callousness and lack of regard for people with illnesses and disabilities
    b. are so seldom performed that they are of little relevance to an understanding of Tiv culture
  * c. use laughter to overcome the Tiv's fear and horror of disease and disability
    d. can be easily written down in a way that conveys the essence of their performed qualities and meanings
    e. all of the above
    f. none of the above

14. Legends:
    a. are traditional stories told by people as if they were true
    b. change plots but not characters
    c. work to reinforce cultural notions of appropriate behavior
    d. express cultural beliefs and values
    e. all of the above
  * f. all of the above except _____(b)

15. Proverbs:
    a. work to minimize deviation from cultural norms
    b. encapsulate cultural wisdom and temper it with wit
    c. succinctly convey the entire idea of a culturally approved behavior
    d. can be used as an informal means of maintaining social control
  * e. all of the above
    f. all of the above except _____

16. Which sentence is *not* true?
    a. The only way that a nonliterate people can preserve and use their myths is by telling and performing them.
    b. The Tiv creation story holds that the world was created by a distant God who took no further interest in it.
    c. The creation story of the Judeo-Christian religions holds the world was created by a God in six days.
    d. The creation story of the Dayak holds that the cosmos began as an entity in the mouth of a coiled water snake.
    e. The Aranda say that the sky and the earth have existed for all of eternity.
  * f. In order to properly serve the members of a given culture, myths must be factually and historically accurate.

17. When studying myths:
    a. anthropologists see beliefs as components that fit together
    b. most scholars agree about what the symbols of a myth mean
    c. most scholars agree that myths must be differentiated from legends
    d. anthropologists often become confused about whether the people telling the myth find it valid
    e. all of the above
  * f. all of the above except _____(b)

18. The dream time of the Aranda:
    a. is connected and interwoven with present-day reality
    b. provides a blueprint for living that emphasizes continuity and connection with the past
    c. creates a living landscape dotted with rocks and trees that embody ancestral beings
    d. suggests that contemporary people are manifestations of their ancestors
  * e. all of the above
    f. all of the above except ____

19. The purposes of ritual can include:
    a. curing the ill
    b. marking a life course event
    c. imploring the spirits for assistance
    d. giving thanks for graces received
    e. effecting a transition for an individual or group
  * f. all of the above

20. The three stages common to most rites of passage include:
    a. prohibition, inhibition, and intensification
    b. chanting, praying, and giving thanks
  * c. separation, transition, integration
    d. praying, healing, and dancing
    e. standing, kneeling, and lying down
    f. none of the above

21. The Isoma ritual of the Ndembu of Zambia:
    a. is performed to cure infertility
    b. aims to restore the woman's good standing with her matrilineal kin group
    c. is fraught with symbols
    d. conveys an idea of chaos
    e. all of the above
  * f. all of the above except ____(d)

22. Gisu male initiation:
    a. requires that the boys must stand absolutely still with no visible expression at all as the circumcision is performed
    b. is barbaric and cruel
    c. serves to separate boys from femininity
    d. concerns the youths' relationships with ancestors only
    e. all of the above
  * f. ____ and ____ (a and c)

Essay

1. Bohannan states, "Cultural life is a process not merely of using tools and meanings but of creatively improving whatever tools we find inadequate and reinterpreting the ideas we find unclear or limiting." From your own life experience, describe a specific example of this process.

2. Using specific examples, discuss the relationship between stories, recontexting, and play.

3. What roles do stories play in the study of history? in religion? art? drama? politics? business? daily life? Elaborate on this subject, using specific examples.

4. What does Bohannan mean when he says "stories recontext the familiar events of living"? Use specific examples in your explanation.

5. How are stories like and unlike play? like and unlike life? What do those similarities and differences have to do with the essential roles stories have played across cultures and throughout human history?

6. Explain the differences, however slight, between folktales, myths, and legends.

7. Write down as many proverbs as you can think of from any culture with which you are very familiar. Then extrapolate from all of them to describe that culture's values, norms, and approved behaviors.

8. Why are jokes funny?

9. In the book, Bohannan gives an example of a Tiv folktale about the vulva that means different things to Tiv women and men. Can you think of a parallel example for American culture?

10. Why do today's feminists take offense at the Tiv folktale about the vulva? Would Tiv women agree with them? Tiv men? What does all this teach us about what happens when we recontext folktales from one culture to another?

11. Briefly describe two or three of your favorite folktales, and see if you can come up with an explicit description of the cultural values they question or express.

12. Name three well-known folktales, and describe the cultural role options presented to children through these tales.

13. Consider the several versions of the Mexican-American story of the weeping woman as described by Bohannan. What morals can you see in each of these versions? What cultural behaviors are discouraged or reinforced?

14. Write down any four well-known American proverbs. What values do they convey? What do these proverbs have to do with social norms?

15. Pick any two myths with which you are familiar, and pinpoint and analyze the differences in the core cultural ideas and values these two myths charter. (Remember that many subcultural groups, including even some anthropology departments, have their own creation stories which are told and retold.)

16. What is the difference between the two kinds of truth recognized by the Tiv? Which kind is truer? By what criteria? Can you point to a parallel example in American culture? How might the Tiv help us out with our notions of "truth"?

17. Are myths true or false? In what sense? Does it matter? Why or why not?

18. See if you can think of two or three specific examples of the recontexting of myth in American life.

19. Compare and contrast Dayak, Aranda, and _____ (a culture or subculture of your choosing) myths in terms of content, form, function, and context.

20. How is the Aranda notion of dream time different from the Judeo-Christian notion of heaven? What behavioral differences do you think this difference in mythologies might be related to?

21. What do myth and ritual have to do with each other? Give specific examples.

22. Does the Ndembu Isoma ritual *really* cure infertility? What is the treatment for infertility in contemporary American society? Does it *really* cure infertility? Which is the most meaningful? Why? Do you think there is any correspondence between the meaningfulness of a ritual and its efficacy at curing? Explain.

23. Why is Gisu circumcision performed without anesthetic? Does this seem to you to be a barbarous custom? Can you draw any parallels between Gisu circumcision and male initiation rites in American culture? Describe. Do any common patterns or underlying values emerge?

Creed
Religion and Ideology

12

What students should get out of the chapter . . .

Human beings explain the universe as they perceive it. Their explanations are their worldview. Religion and science are both parts of any worldview, and are not necessarily contradictory. Science focuses on questions and ways to improve those questions—science is as good as its questions. Religion focuses on faith and security, and is as good as its answers. Ideologies, whether political or other, more often shared the characteristics of religion than of science.

Films and Videos

Holy Ghost People. 53 min. black and white. 1967. University of California Extension Media Center. Remarkable record of a white Pentecostal religious group in Appalachia whose members handle poisonous snakes, drink strychnine, and speak in tongues, following the literal interpretation of a Biblical passage. During a four-hour meeting the congregation is exhorted by an evangelist, and members tell of revelations they have experienced through communication with the Holy Ghost. Some speak in tongues or collapse in trancelike states. We see a leader bitten by a rattlesnake at the height of a meeting, and the film ends with his hand and arm swelling.

India's Sacred Cow. 28 min. color. 1980. Indiana University Audio-Visual Center. Investigates the importance of domestic cattle to the Indian people, especially the Hindus. Explains that the Hindu tradition forbids its followers to kill cows or to eat their food, but Hindus may consume the cow's milk and cheese, and use the cow's dung as fuel and fertilizer. Observes that, since cows are sacred, many shrines are built to "Mother Cow" and the cows are allowed to wander unharmed throughout the towns and cities.

Latah: A Culture-Specific Elaboration of the Startle Reflex. 39 min. color. 1983. Indiana University Audio-Visual Center. Examines the clearly defined social role developed in a Malaysian culture for individuals who startle strongly and easily. These latahs, as they are called, are typically older females who, when repeatedly startled, become agitated to a trancelike state. When in this latah state, they may say things that are otherwise taboo, obey forcefully given commands no matter how extreme, or match the behaviors of others no matter how foolish.

The Lion Hunters. 68 min. color. 1970. University of California Extension Media Center. Ethnographic classic shows men of Niger who hunt lion with bow and arrow. Explains why hunters are a group apart from their fellow kin, and captures elaborate ceremonial preparations and intricacies of brewing poison for arrows. Follows action through to the kill. Filmed by noted documentarian Jean Rouch.

Witchcraft among the Azande. 52 min. color. 1982. Penn State Audio-Visual Services. Focuses on the practice of witchcraft among the African Azande people who depend upon oracles to explain events and to predict the future. Shows an adultery trial in which a ritually-poisoned chicken decides the outcome. Highlights the tribe's conflict and compromise between modernity and tradition, and between Christianity and magic.

Chapter 12

Test Items

True/False

1. Some peoples' worldview is so deeply merged with their perceptions of the natural world that the eternal questions need never be asked. T

2. In Western culture, the answers to the eternal questions provided by science always conflict with those provided by religion. F

3. While science tends to focus on questions, religion tends to focus on answers. T

4. Many Americans conjoin a combination of religious and scientific elements in their individual worldviews. T

5. When an individual deeply believes in a certain religion, it is usually very easy for him or her to accept the validity of other religions. F

6. A fundamental error made by many early missionaries was to assume not only that their religion was the only true one, but also that the ideas underlying their worldviews were the only valid ones. T

7. A fundamental error made by early scholars of primitive religion was to assume that all primitive religions were different. F

8. Anthropologists can best understand religion by assuming that religion and culture are separate and treating them as distinct realms of inquiry. F

9. Religion can be usefully studied by anthropologists as a way of looking at how people search for meaning in the eternal questions. T

10. Religions work to reinforce social groups, establish codes of good behavior, and provide comfort to people in adversity. T

11. The usual means of communicating information to the higher spirits include revelation, divination, possession and drugs. F

12. In the Dinka ritual, the person presenting the prayer is confessing his own guilt to the spirit. F

13. When the Dinka pray for the health of one individual, they are also reaffirming the unity of the social group. T

14. The ritual sacrifice of an ox during a Dinka curing ceremony is meant to exchange the life of the ox for the life of the sick individual. T

15. Like Judaism, Christianity, and Islam, all religions postulate revelation that was provided in the past and can be worked with in the present. F

16. Oracles reinforce scientific answers to questions concerning misfortunes and illness. F

17. Oracles are a means of divination not found in contemporary American society. F

18. Vodou possession seems to its practitioners to provide constant and easy communication between humans and spirits. T

19. The use of drugs in communicating with the divine is limited to a few geographical areas. F

20. Early Spanish priests confronted with the Aztec religious use of peyote were astonished at its inspirational power and sought to foster and encourage its use. **F**

21. The Huichol of northwestern Mexico use peyote as a unifying symbol of their hunting and gathering past and their agricultural present. **T**

22. The primary characteristic of the shaman is the ability to directly experience the supernatural. **T**

23. Charismatic Christian preachers have little in common with traditional shamans. **F**

24. All religions are based on the premise that humans are the designated beneficiaries of the environment. **F**

25. Early British colonists were astonished at the complexity and beauty of the aboriginal religions. **F**

26. The Australian notion of dream time postulates a sharp separation between humans and their environment, and between past and future. **F**

27. The primary goal of Australian aborigines was progress, growth, and change. **F**

28. The premises of Australian aboriginal religion are very much in keeping with the values and goals of the American environmental movement. **T**

29. The underlying premises of Navajo religion involve harmony, reciprocity, and beauty. **T**

30. Navajo believe that when people deviate from the correct way, harmony and beauty must be ritually restored. **T**

31. The Navajo do not practice rituals. **F**

32. If you accept the basic premise of witchcraft that misfortune is caused by the ill will of other people, it is a logical set of beliefs. **T**

33. Navajo believe that the sand paintings designed by witches are helpful in curing the victim of an illness. **F**

34. Religions can be usefully studied as designs for living, among other things. **T**

35. Buddhism as a design for living encourages people to lead moral and charitable lives so they can reincarnate in a better position in the next life. **T**

36. Most Buddhists do not accept Buddhism as a practical design for living, but try instead to withdraw from the world and seek the blissful and eternal nothingness of nirvana. **F**

37. Religion answers more or less the same questions everywhere. **T**

38. Cults and ideologies are the same as religions. **F**

39. An ideology is a set of doctrines, assertions, and intentions that underlie a social or political movement. **T**

40. Ideologies tend to be more concerned with spiritual matters than with changing the power dimensions of a given society. **F**

41. Ideology is similar to religion in that it calls for faith over inquiry. **T**

42. Science as practiced is entirely objective and free from the constraining influence of ideology. **F**

43. Cults are often said by their members to be religions. **T**

44. Cults are organizations that are disapproved of by almost everyone except their members. **T**

45. Cults never develop into full-fledged organized religions.   F

46. Cults often supply answers not only to the eternal questions but also to many personal decisions and details of their members' lives.   T

47. Cults never help anyone; they only do harm.   F

48. Cults have provided many Americans with ways to remove themselves from the larger society and its problems and dangers.   T

49. We must be careful not to let ideologies, which help to simplify complex choices, stop all inquiry and stultify growth.   T

Multiple Choice

1. An individual's worldview:
   a. is the same as his or her religion
   b. is often so deeply merged with his or her perception of the natural world that the eternal questions need never be asked
   c. can be an amalgam of science, religion, and other elements
   d. is totally determined by the culture
   e. all of the above
   * f. ____ and ____ (b and c)

2. The answers provided by religion and science to the eternal questions:
   a. necessarily conflict
   b. are usually the same
   * c. offer elements that individuals can choose from to construct their unique worldviews
   d. are always based on the faith of the questioning individual
   e. none of the above

3. According to Bohannan, although "having faith" in a religion means that inquiry must sometimes be foregone, the advantages include:
   a. immense psychological security
   b. a strong and reassuring sense of social predictability and group cohesion
   c. emotional comfort and a sense of meaning, even in adversity
   d. a clear design for living in a confusing world
   * e. all of the above
   f. all of the above except ____

4. Early missionaries:
   a. tended to assume that the native religions they encountered were designs for living uniquely adapted to the environment of that group, and were therefore worthy of study and respect
   b. tended to accept native religions as providing answers to the eternal questions equally as valid as those of Christianity
   c. invented concepts like totemism and animism to explain primitive religions in terms Westerners could understand
   * d. assumed that the ideas underlying their own worldviews were the only possible and correct ones
   e. all of the above
   f. ____ and ____

111

5. Early scholars of primitive religion:
   a. were careful to ask only those questions of primitive religions that they would ask of their own
   * b. tried to interpret all primitive religions as if all "primitive" groups were alike
   c. conducted detailed ethnographic investigations of each primitive group in order to understand each religion in the unique terms and environmental circumstances of the culture that it served
   d. understood that for many groups, religion was not separate from everyday life
   e. all of the above

6. Anthropological concepts like totemism and magic:
   a. are useful in the interpretation and understanding of all primitive religions
   b. clarify the religious categories and practices of some peoples, while obscuring those of other peoples
   c. were applied by early scholars to the religions of many tribal peoples where they had no real relevance or usefulness
   d. reflect a sort of academic ethnocentrism similar to the religious ethnocentrism of the early missionaries
   e. all of the above
   * f. all of the above except _____ (a)

7. Religion can be usefully studied by anthropologists as:
   a. a design or blueprint for living
   b. a way of searching for meaning
   c. a basis for reinforcing the cohesion of a given social group
   d. a device for providing comfort to people in adversity
   * e. all of the above
   f. a and c only

8. Information is usually communicated to the spiritual realm by humans through:
   * a. prayer, invocation, and sacrifice
   b. separation, transition, and incorporation
   c. revelation, divination, possession, and drugs
   d. supplication, suffering, and sin
   e. all of the above

9. When the Dinka of the Sudan ritually sacrifice an ox during a curing ritual:
   a. they are symbolically communicating with the spirit world
   b. they are placing their entire belief system in jeopardy if the patient dies, as his death would show that their rituals do not work
   c. they are seeking to substitute the life of the ox for the life of the sick individual
   d. they are asserting and reinforcing the unity of the community
   e. all of the above
   * f. all of the above except _____ (b)

10. Humans usually get information out of the spiritual realm through:
    * a. revelation, possession, divination, and drugs
    b. prayer, invocation, and sacrifice
    c. chanting and dancing
    d. witches, sorcerers, and wizards
    e. all of the above

11. Judaism, Christianity, and Islam are primarily religions of:
    a. divination
    b. possession
    * c. revelation
    d. oracles
    e. drugs

12. Which sentence is true?
    * a. Divination and oracles provide information from the realm of the divine on a case-by-case basis.
    b. Using divination and oracles to get information out of the divine is an example of superstitious behavior.
    c. Oracles rarely answer questions involving everyday life.
    d. Oracles can only answer questions that science and logic could answer.

13. Possession by spirits is anthropologically viewed as:
    a. happening to individuals with weak spirits
    b. the work of the devil
    * c. a mode of acquiring information from the supernatural
    d. a way to attract tourists to poor countries
    e. all of the above
    f. all of the above except _____

14. Huichol religion:
    a. uses peyote as a unifying symbol of the hunting/gathering past and the agricultural present
    b. interprets the hallucinations induced by peyote as evidence of the divine
    c. is not considered to be separate from everyday life
    d. was destroyed in the 1600s by the Spanish Inquisition
    e. all of the above
    * f. all of the above except _____(d)

15. Shamans:
    a. can directly experience the supernatural and communicate with the spirit(s) without the use of intermediary techniques
    b. often serve as a doorway between the human and supernatural realms
    c. both become possessed by the spirits and can possess them
    d. uses drugs to traverse the boundary between the spiritual and human worlds
    * e. all of the above
    f. all of the above except _____

113

16. Which sentence is true?
    a. A basic premise underlying the religion of the Aranda aborigines of Australia is that humans have a place in the environment very much like that of other creatures.
    b. The basic premises underlying the religion of the Navajo involve harmony, reciprocity, and beauty.
    c. A basic premise underlying Buddhism is that there is no virtue in personal reward.
    d. A basic premise underlying the religion of the Tiv is that human beings contain within themselves all the sources of evil, as well as of good.
  * e. All of the above.

17. The Navajo belief in witchcraft:
    a. is an irrational example of primitive thinking
  * b. follows logically from the premises that there must be strict reciprocity between humans and the supernatural and that misfortune is caused by the ill will of others
    c. states that, once disrupted, the harmonious and beautiful balance of the universe cannot be restored
    d. entails reliance on sand paintings to do ill to others
    e. all of the above except ____

18. Buddhism as a design for living:
    a. is inflexible, requiring great personal sacrifice in the effort to extinguish personal desire
    b. has enough flexibility to allow its adherents to achieve ample personal rewards, in spite of its basic premise that there is no virtue in personal reward
    c. encourages people to lead moral lives in an attempt to improve their position on the wheel of life next time around
    d. is easily accommodated to the premises of other religions
    e. all of the above
  * f. all of the above except ____ (a)

19. Ideologies:
    a. are sets of doctrines, assertions, and intentions that underlie social or political movements
    b. often provide answers to the eternal questions
    c. usually have as their purpose changing the power dimensions of society
    d. blend with religion when religion is used as a blueprint for political action
    e. generally call for faith over inquiry
  * f. all of the above

20. The label cult is generally applied to:
  * a. minority religious organizations that are generally discredited by everyone but their members
    b. small religious sects that accept the norms of society
    c. established religions by the priests of other religions
    d. proponents of political ideologies
    e. none of the above

21. Christianity and Mormonism are examples of:
    a. contemporary American cults
    b. primitive animistic religions
    c. political ideologies
  * d. full-fledged organized religions that began as cults
    e. none of the above

22. The Church of Scientology, Rev. Moon's Unification Church, and the Hare Krishnas are all examples of:
    a. established and culturally-recognized religions
    b. religious sects
  * c. contemporary American groups labelled cults by the wider society
    d. charismatic Christian spinoffs from Protestant churches

23. Advantages of cult membership for some individuals include:
    a. relief from the pressures of daily life
    b. the security of membership in a close-knit group
    c. the discipline of strict regimens
    d. designs for living that mark a clear path through the maze of contemporary society
  * e. all of the above
    f. all of the above except _____

24. Science:
    a. provides a moral element
    b. provides built-in answers to difficult questions
  * c. continually provides good questions
    d. can cause imprisonment in cultural traps
    e. _____ and _____

Essay

1. What are the primary differences between science and religion? Describe the advantages and disadvantages of each relative to the other. Do you prefer one mode over the other? Must one choose?

2. What was the problem with early scholarly investigations of primitive religion? What have we learned from their mistakes, and how has that problem been resolved by later generations of anthropologists?

3. What does any viable religion do for its adherents?

4. Is there a difference between culture and religion? Discuss, using specific examples.

5. If the Dinka of the Sudan sacrifice an ox to save the life of a sick individual, and the patient dies anyway, do they then lose faith in their religious system? Why or why not?

6. Bohannan states that humans in general communicate with the divine by putting information into the system and getting information out of the system. Give specific examples of each process from other cultures besides your own, and then contrast each example with a parallel example from a mainstream American religion.

115

7. a. Discuss the cross-cultural use of oracles, using specific examples.

   b. What kinds of oracles are available in contemporary American culture? Do you ever consult oracles? Do you know anyone who does? What sort of information do oracles give? What is the value of such information? Can it be obtained any other way?

8. Interpret vodou possession in the context of Haitian society and worldview.

9. Why is peyote so important to the Huichol of northwestern Mexico? What specifically do you think might happen to Huichol religion and culture if their use of peyote were to be outlawed by the Mexican government?

10. What are shamans? What makes them different from priests? Why have they been such important figures in so many cultures and religions around the world?

11. a. What philosophical premises underlie the religions of (pick any three) the Aranda aborigines of Australia? the Navajo? the Dinka? the Huichol? Buddhism? Christianity? Judaism? What behaviors follow logically from each of these premises?

   b. Now pick a religion not discussed in the book, and see if you can identify its basic premises and their behavioral ramifications.

12. Why do the Navajo and the Tiv believe in witchcraft? Is such belief an example of rational thinking? Why or why not?

13. How can Buddhism be a "design for living" when its basic premises would seem to lead logically to the conclusion that people should withdraw from social life?

14. What is the difference between a religion and a cult? Do cults ever become religions? Do religions ever become cults? Discuss, using specific examples.

15. List as many cults that exist or have existed in the U.S. as you can think of. What do they have in common? Why are they pejoratively labelled "cults" instead of "religions"? What advantages do such groups offer their members? What are their drawbacks? State and explain your personal opinion of such groups.

16. What does Bohannan say is the problem with the easy answers to the eternal questions provided by cults? Do you agree? Are cults ever useful for particular individuals? Explain.

17. Reread the eternal questions Bohannan poses on the first page of Chapter 12. Write down your own individual answers to these questions. Then pretend you are an anthropologist whose job is to come up with a succinct description of your worldview: its roots in your culture and personal past, its basic premises, and the design for living it suggests.

Now take a critical look at this worldview you have described. Are these the beliefs you want to hold? Why or why not? If they are not, how might what you have learned about cultural anthropology help you alter them? If they are, how can you reinforce them so that they will retain their vitality in you?

Conclude your essay by describing what, if anything, you have learned from this exercise.

[NOTE TO INSTRUCTOR: If you use this question, we recommend that you make it optional, not required.]

Part Four

MEANING

1. What does "the human capacity for symbolization" mean? What do symbols have to do with art? with language? with play?

2. Describe the essential qualities of art, of play, and of creativity.

3. Explain Bohannan's concept of recontexting. What does recontexting have to do with myth and religion? Use specific examples in your discussion.

4. Discuss the relationships between language, art, and ethnocentrism, using specific examples from your own experience.

5. What does Bohannan mean when he says that language is power? Could the same be said of performance? Discuss, using specific examples.

6. Consider the role of art and symbol in religion, using specific examples.

7. What does it mean to say that religion is a "design for living"? Pick any religion, and show how that religion provides a design for living. In your discussion, pay specific attention to its myths, rituals, symbols, as well as to its recontexting of elements from other aspects of the culture.

8. What is a story? Why are stories told in every known human culture? Evaluate the role of stories in art and religion, using specific examples.

9. Discuss the relationship of story, art, and performance to the eternal questions.

10. Evaluate the role of language in the shaping of worldview.

11. What do myths have to do with story? with ritual? with performance? with creativity?

12. Given that myths charter the cultural world as it is currently set up, would it be true to say that they stifle creativity? Discuss, using specific examples.

13. Make up a myth, and ritual(s) to enact it.
    a. Describe the culture chartered by the myth in some detail (include subsistence method, political and economic system, gender relations, social structure, worldview).
    b. Now write a story about a cult that spins off from the mainstream culture you described above. Describe its myths and rituals and the worldview they foster. How does the cult differ from mainstream religion in terms of all the categories you considered above (subsistence method, etc.)? How do you know it is a cult, and not another religion? Why does it arise? Why are some people attracted to it? What good does it do? What problems does it cause?
    c. Conclude your story in a way that demonstrates the relationship between cults, religions, the eternal questions, and membership in society.

How Culture Works

13

What students should get out of the chapter . . .

To see how culture works, we turn from its substantive aspects to its verbal aspects—from culture as a noun to culture as a verb. Action chains—events that follow one another in a pattern—must be understood if social traps are to be avoided. Some action chains are cycles; others are trajectories.

Culture can be changed by invention, diffusion, and recontexting. Evolution results when culture is sufficiently altered that people cannot go back to what they did before the changes occurred.

Europe's cultural growth (and its particular values and ideas) led to immense expansion in the years following 1400. The social inventions first of mercantilism, then of capitalism (then, as we shall see later, of the socialisms) has impacted the entire globe.

Films and Videos

Dance and Human History. 40 min. color. 1976. University of California Extension Media Center. Introduction to the work of Alan Lomax and his colleagues in developing choreometrics, a cross-cultural method of studying the relationship of dance style to social structure. Analyzing dance films from all over the world, the group compared dances cross-culturally and established a connection between patterns of movement and patterns of culture.

Step Style. 29 min. color. 1980. University of California Extension Media Center. Fascinating cross-cultural study of leg and foot movements in dance styles throughout the world. The various step styles illustrated are shown to be related to productive activities, social structure, and so on. The longitudinal foot-crossing step common in Eurasia, for example, mirrors the heel-to-toe stride of the plowman; dances that emphasize lower leg agility and the pointing of heel and toe are shown to be typical of highly stratified, socially complex cultures, where lower leg activity is crucial in establishing social distance and levels.

Chapter 13

Test Items

True/False

1. A gene pool is the collection of all the genes available in a given population. **T**

2. A culture pool is the totality of culture within an interacting population. **T**

3. Order in an action chain does not matter. **F**

4. A change in the order of actions in an action chain is analogous to learning in the individual. **T**

5. Action chains have to do with social events, while event chains focus on the actions of the actors. **F**

6. Action chains can form either cycles or trajectories. **T**

7. An action chain can imprison its actors in a social trap when they do not have enough culture to devise a way out of what appears to be an inevitable series of actions and reprisals. **T**

8. The corporation, the clan, and the steam engine are all examples of social inventions. **F**

9. Both technological and social inventiveness are necessarily limited by cultural preconditions. **T**

10. The main criteria for the acceptance of an invention is based on who invented it, not whether conditions are right. **F**

11. The process by which elements of culture spread across geography is called invention. **F**

12. It is in the nature of human culture to remain static. **F**

13. Important culture crests in human history include the development of agriculture, the rise of mercantilism, and the Industrial Revolution. **T**

14. Evolution only refers to biology, not to culture. **F**

15. Cultural evolution means that the members of a given culture cannot go back to earlier ways. **T**

16. Biological evolution involves genetic losses and gains. **T**

17. Cultural evolution involves the invention of new culture but never the loss of old culture. **F**

18. Money, agriculture, and computers are not examples of cultural evolutionary steps. **F**

19. Culture change is a rare phenomenon occurring only very occasionally over the long course of human history. **F**

20. Culture crests involve the accumulation of many small changes into what often seems to be the appearance of totally new patterns. **T**

21. The peoples of the precolonial world lived in complete isolation from one another. **F**

22. Early anthropologists were fully aware that contact and change were characteristic of most human cultures throughout human history. **F**

23. The expansion of Europe was made possible by technological inventions alone. **F**

24. Christopher Columbus was a map maker trained in Holland. **T**

25. Mercantile capitalism assumed that the state was the only organization with enough power, resources, and information to finance and regulate trade. **T**

26. Mercantile capitalism used paper money as the fundamental measure of wealth. **F**

27. Mercantilists viewed global resources and wealth as unlimited and infinitely expandable. **F**

28. The social trap of mercantilism lay in its attempts to share the world's resources equally among all nations. **F**

29. The Iberians sought both to corner the wealth of the New World and to Christianize all its peoples. **T**

30. The colonial response to the widespread decimation and death of Native American peoples was to adopt a more enlightened policy toward Native Americans to keep them from dying out completely. **F**

31. The colonial response to the widespread decimation and death of Native American peoples was to import African slaves to replace their labor. **T**

32. There was little significant difference between capitalism and mercantilism. **F**

33. While the mercantilist system characterized the economic colonialism of the English, Dutch, and French, capitalism characterized the economic colonialism of the Iberians. **F**

34. The differences between the mercantilist and capitalist systems go a long way toward explaining the greater abilities of the English, Dutch, and French to take advantage of the cultural innovations of the Industrial Revolution. **T**

35. Joint-stock companies often carried out legal and warfare functions on contract with the governments. **T**

36. The essence of capitalism is allowing the central government to set prices and to set policy. **F**

37. Even after the advent of capitalism, householding remained the basic form of economy in Western Europe. **F**

38. Capitalism subjected both labor and land to the same market forces as raw materials and products. **T**

39. One of the most momentous changes in human history occurred when working for a wage became the only way to get the wherewithal to live. **T**

40. Mercantilism returned as an alternative to capitalism to help reduce human misery. **F**

41. Unrestricted capitalism turned out to work best for rich and poor alike. **F**

Multiple Choice

1. Culture pools and gene pools:
    a. become fixed and immutable
    b. always die out over time
  * c. expand and retract as individual persons travel or migrate
    d. are not really comparable in a scientific sense
    e. all of the above
    f. none of the above

2. Strips of action or events, seen from the standpoint of the actors, are called:
   a. event chains
   * b. action chains
   c. social traps
   d. performances
   e. none of the above

3. Action chains:
   a. most often require at least two people
   b. involve doing things in the "right" order
   c. are social processes when they involve more than one person
   d. can differ between subgroups within one culture
   * e. all of the above
   f. all of the above except _____

4. Action chains become social traps when they:
   * a. are followed uncritically
   b. are followed creatively and adapted to new circumstances
   c. turn into event chains
   d. become cycles instead of trajectories
   e. all of the above
   f. none of the above

5. Examples of action chains that turned into social traps include:
   a. feuds
   b. duels
   c. warfare between the Greek city-states
   d. hunting and gathering
   e. all of the above
   * f. all of the above except _____ (d)

6. Social traps can be detected and ameliorated by:
   * a. human creativity
   b. nothing—once you're in one, there's no way out
   c. colonialism
   d. mercantilism
   e. capitalism

7. The fact that culture is a system means that:
   a. parts can be separated out and changed without changing the whole
   b. to change one part puts all the rest under stress
   c. entire cultures can be threatened by sudden environmental changes
   d. human inventiveness and creativity are often summoned to help cultures cope with the stress of change
   e. all of the above
   * f. all of the above except _____ (a)

8. Examples of social inventions already accomplished include:
   a. the clan
   b. the state
   c. the publicly-owned corporation
   d. institutions that can successfully clean up the environment and solve the problems of poverty and homelessness
   e. all of the above
 * f. all of the above except _____ (d)

9. Creating and implementing new social institutions:
 * a. requires changes in a culture's basic social values
   b. involves few alterations to the status quo
   c. is unrelated to profit incentive
   d. requires advanced technology
   e. does not depend on preconditions

10. Social and technological inventions:
   a. only succeed if they are first taken up by the wealthy
   b. can take root at any level in society
   c. can spread between cultures through diffusion
   d. are rarely re-invented once they are rejected
   e. all of the above
 * f. _____ and _____ (b and c)

11. A culture crest:
   a. is a fundamental turning point in the growth and development of a culture
   b. results from the gradual accumulation of small cultural changes
   c. can result from significant advances in technology
   d. is often experienced by the members of a culture as bringing rapid and overwhelming change
 * e. all of the above
   f. all of the above except _____

12. Examples of culture crests include or will most likely include:
   a. the transition from hunting and gathering to agriculture
   b. the global mercantile empires of Western Europe
   c. the Industrial Revolution
   d. social change resulting from the technologies, discoveries and opportunities created by space travel
 * e. all of the above
   f. all of the above except _____

13. Cultural evolution:
    a. involves overcoming opposing forces and opening up new options
    b. has taken place when a cultural change makes it impossible to go back to the way things were before the change occurred
    c. is a cyclical process like the laying of the egg and the hatching of the chicken
    d. involves the addition of new genetic material and the loss of old genetic material
    e. all of the above
  * f. all of the above except ____ and ____ (c and d)

14. Anthropologists up until about 1960 thought that most of the peoples of the world before the colonial expansion of Europe:
    a. experienced no culture contact or change
    b. lived in distinct and separate cultures
    c. were interconnected through trade routes that spanned continents and oceans and dispersed culture as well as goods
    d. seemed static by comparison to the culture crest in Europe during mercantilism
  * e. ____ and ____ (a and b)

15. The European culture crest in the 1400s:
    a. was made possible by the technical improvements in sailing technology
    b. depended on the social invention known as mercantile capitalism
    c. fortified the estate system
    d. changed the entire world
    e. all of the above
  * f. all of the above except ____ (c)

16. Some fundamental assumptions made by mercantilism included the notions that:
    a. the state was the only organization with enough power, resources, and information to finance and regulate trade
    b. finite resources like gold, silver, and jewels were the only measure of wealth
    c. the aim of trade and exploration was to enrich the treasury of the state
    d. the world's wealth grew fastest when shared among nations
    e. one nation could only become wealthy at the expense of another
  * f. all of the above except ____ (d)

17. Hand-in-hand with the European desire to corner all the world's wealth went the European desire to:
    a. bring peace and prosperity to all the world's peoples
    b. design a new economic system that gave political autonomy to colonized nations
    c. learn as much as possible about the traditional cultures of subjugated peoples
  * d. Christianize all the world's peoples
    e. all of the above

127

18. The colonialist endeavors of Holland, England, and France:
    a. took the same form as those of Spain and Portugal
    b. differed dramatically from those of Spain and Portugal
    c. utilized a cultural innovation called capitalism
    d. always relied on the central government to finance large-scale expeditions
  * e. _____ and _____ (b and c)
    f. all of the above

19. Dutch, English, and French joint-stock companies:
    a. were ongoing business organizations
    b. were owned by many people, each of whom held some shares in the enterprise
    c. minimized individual risk, while maximizing capital
    d. were always entirely separate from the state, and carried out only economic enterprises
    e. all of the above
  * f. all of the above except _____ (d)

20. Capitalism:
    a. involves allowing the choices of purchasers and producers to set prices and policy
    b. meant that for the first time in human history, land and labor became commodities to be bought, sold, and traded in the market
    c. involves a *laissez faire* policy
    d. contains within it still unsolved social traps for the poor and the unemployed
  * e. all of the above
    f. all of the above except _____

21. Which of the following is *not* one of the controlling ideas of capitalism?
    a. self-interest is the servant of society
    b. the role of government in business should be minimized
    c. private property is sacrosanct
    d. religious salvation is associated with worldly success
  * e. the needs of the many should take precedence over the profits of the few

22. Which of the following is *not* one of the problems resulting from unrestricted capitalism?
    a. economic instability and business cycles of boom and bust that arise from lags in supply and demand
    b. gross inequality in the distribution of wealth
  * c. a restrictive, caste-like social system that does not allow for social mobility
    d. neglect of the public interest
    e. poverty, homelessness, and unemployment

23. The world is still waiting for new social inventions that will allow people to amass enough capital to:

    a. clean up the environment

    b. insure good health care for everyone

    c. run a complex economy and still assure the welfare of all

    d. guarantee a good education to all citizens

 * e. all of the above

    f. _____ and _____

Essay

1. At the beginning of Chapter 13, Bohannan states, "Using an analogy to computers, we can see that culture is a bank of information in the sense of data. It is also information in the sense of the program in the software that organizes, manipulates and uses the data." Draw out this analogy as far as you can, using as many specific examples as possible.

2. What do social traps have to do with event and action chains? Discuss, using specific examples.

3. Name at least three specific examples of historical action chains that led to social traps, explain what culture was lacking, and then devise sufficient culture, as appropriate to that historical period as you can make it, that could have gotten the actors out of their social traps and so altered the course of history.

4. Give two examples of action chains that form trajectories, and two examples of action chains that form cycles.

5. According to Bohannan, both technological and social types of inventiveness are limited by cultural preconditions. Give two examples of such limitation from history. What do you see being invented today that cannot be used because our culture is not ready?

6. In Chapter 13, Bohannan states that acceptance of some inventions depends on who first takes up the new invention. From your own knowledge of American culture, name and discuss at least two examples of inventions which were first accepted by different levels of society. Did the usage change as acceptance diffused to other levels?

7. How do people get new culture? Discuss, using specific examples.

8. Explain Bohannan's notion of a culture crest. Give several examples of culture crests, at least two of which should not come from the Bohannan text but from your own review of history. Did these culture crests result in cultural evolution? How do you know?

9. According to Bohannan, a true evolutionary step occurs when a biological or cultural change makes it impossible to go back to the way things were before the change occurred. Give three examples of cultural evolutionary steps, and explain why, in each case, it became impossible to go back to the way things were.

10. From the information that Columbus was a map maker trained in Holland who saw Iceland in his youth, what can you deduce about the European world in Columbus' time?

11. Why were slaves brought into the New World?

12. What made the colonial expansion of Western Europe happen when it did?

13. a. If the prevailing ideology of Western Europe during what we know as the colonial period had included the notions that the powerful are responsible for insuring the welfare of the weak, and that wealth for any nation arises from healthy trade that benefits all, would history be different? How might the world look today?

    b. Given that Christianity was the prevailing religion of the time, would such an ideology have been theoretically possible? Why or why not?

14. Why were the English, French, and Dutch colonizers able to take greater advantage of the cultural innovations of the Industrial Revolution than the Iberians? What difference did that make in today's world?

15. What are the major differences between the mercantilist and capitalist systems? What were the effects of those differences on colonized countries?

16. What were the basic ideas behind early capitalism? How did those ideas have to be modified, and who did the modifying? Is modern capitalism a perfect system, or does it contain social traps? Explain your answers, using specific examples.

17. What social inventions do we need today? Why? Design one or more of the inventions that you feel we need. Explain why it (they) would work better than what currently exists to solve the culture problems you pinpoint. Why won't it (they) catch on immediately? What obstacles would have to be overcome, and what do you see as the possibilities for its (their) success?

From Colonialism
to Global Society

14

What students should get out of the chapter . . .

The speed of expansion of Western society increased in the 1400s and 1500s as Western countries spread out in search of wealth and trade. In the following centuries, all the world's societies were affected. Some perished, others collapsed. Some resisted and adapted, with greater or lesser success. As a result, what we today call the Third World has emerged: these societies have taken over many tools and ideas from Western societies, but in the process have become dependent on those Western societies for machines, fertilizer and the like. Thus, the increased production of the Third World has not led to better living conditions for the people.

Films and Videos

First Contact. 54 min. color. 1983. University of California Extension Media Center. Superb documentary history of the first contacts between white Australians and the "Stone Age" natives of Papua New Guinea in the 1930s. Features extensive "home movie" footage taken at the time as well as interviews with those who still remember the events—from both the native and the Australian point of view. An informative, humorous, and ultimately profound look at the meeting of two alien cultures. Recipient of top international awards.

The Last of the Cuiva. 65 min. color. 1971. Films Incorporated Video. In northeast Colombia, surrounded by the ranches of settlers, live the last of the Cuiva. On land that once was their own there are now cattle and fences to exclude them, and cowboys with their alien culture and their guns. The ranchers say the Cuiva are dangerous and "naked like animals." The Cuiva tell of massacres. Only a very few Cuiva retain their traditional nomadic, hunting and gathering lifestyle. The rest are being drawn more and more into contact with the white ranchers, working as day laborers to earn the money for which they so recently had no use, learning about prostitution, alcoholism, and evangelical religion.

Trobriand Cricket: An Ingenious Response to Colonialism. 54 min. color. 1976. University of California Extension Media Center. Classic ethnographic documentary on the modifications made by the residents of the Trobriand Islands in Papua New Guinea, to the traditional British game of cricket. In an ingenious response to colonialism, the islanders have changed the game into an outlet for mock warfare, community interchange, tribal rivalry, sexual innuendo, and a lot of riotous fun. Recipient of top international awards.

Chapter 14

Test Items

True/False

1. The theory of the great chain of being held that all living creatures were interlinked and interdependent, and therefore equal.   F

2. Europeans of the colonial period held the notion, stemming from the great chain of being, that everyone was equal.   F

3. The concept of the noble savage grew out of the idea that civilized people had fallen from grace.   T

4. The concepts of the noble savage and the great chain of being did much to improve relationships and understanding between colonizers and colonized.   F

5. Reactions of those cultures newly dominated by the expanding European powers ranged from total extinction to adaptation.   T

6. Missionaries were often the only colonizers to believe that the natives were human beings with souls.   T

7. Colonization of indigenous peoples by Europeans occurred in Siberia, North and South America, India, Africa, most of Asia, the East Indies and the Pacific Islands.   T

8. From the point of view of native peoples all over the world, the expansion of the Western colonial powers was cataclysmically disastrous.   T

9. A colony is a group of people living under the political rule of a local and benevolent administrator.   F

10. One benefit of colonialism was that it usually allowed those colonized to define what would be best for them within the colonial system.   F

11. The Tasmanians were noble savages whose childlike innocence was what saved them from the guns and diseases of the colonial settlers.   F

12. Myth and belief played no role at all in the fall of the Aztec empire to Cortes and his followers.   F

13. Most colonized cultures reacted with a pattern of resistance and adaptation.   T

14. Cortes saw himself as the returning god Quetzalcoatl, and acted accordingly in his dealings with the Aztecs.   F

15. The Yaqui of Mexico underwent four near complete changes of culture and still survived as an identifiable cultural group.   T

16. Colonialism for many colonized peoples resulted in extreme cultural dissonance, which they often sought to resolve through religious cults.   T

17. To insiders, cults can be serious attempts to make sense of a senseless world, while to outsiders such cults may appear to be absurd.   T

18. A millenarian cult is one that happens every thousand years.   F

19. The ghost dance expressed the tensions and frustrations felt by many Native Americans and attempted to solve problems that seemed insoluble in the material world. T

20. Cargo cults postulated that the colonists would arrive and share their cargo with the native people. F

21. Native peoples, feeling insecure with their current situation, sometimes went back to cultural practices in earlier times. T

22. Melanesian cargo cults were irrational and petty attempts to gain material benefits for Melanesians. F

23. Millenarian cults can be interpreted as examples of cultural flight. T

24. The term Third World originally referred to those nations that would not join the Cold War by siding with either the capitalist First World or the communist Second World. T

25. The Third World includes about fifty states and a small proportion of the world's population. F

26. The global market economy that resulted from colonialism has effectively narrowed the gap between rich and poor countries, thus benefitting everyone. F

27. Colonialism, in most Third World countries, effectively resulted in an increase in agricultural production *and* an increase in malnutrition. T

28. Neo-colonialism refers to the utilization of the Third World not only for labor and resources, but also as a market for First World goods. T

29. Capitalism has traditionally depended for its success on the existence of a large underclass of exploitable people. T

30. Because of the cultural and regional diversity of the peoples of the Earth, there is no such thing as "planet-wide culture." F

31. It is still possible for a major disaster to strike a country like Japan or Germany without having any serious repercussions on the economies of most other nations. F

32. As global interdependence has grown, cultural diversity has seriously declined. F

33. Most individuals in the U.S. in the 1990s participate in a number of cultures, some part of the time, some almost all the time. T

34. According to Bohannan, the idea of "human rights" is becoming a value in global culture. T

35. A very global concept is that we must enjoy our work. F

36. Because home has become a haven for us today, the norms of family form and function are very clear to us. F

37. A SPIN—a network of equals drawn together by shared interests, purposes, and convictions. T

38. SPINs have no political power and little social or economic importance. F

39. It is still possible today for a nation or a cultural group to live in complete isolation from the rest of the world. F

Multiple Choice

1. Premises that blinded Europeans as they formed their views of natives in the colonized world included:
    a. the great chain of being
    b. the concept of the noble savage
    c. the notion that all peoples are created equal
    d. the concept of the inherent intelligence and superiority of indigenous peoples
    e. all of the above
    * f. _____ and _____ (a and b)

2. The idea of the great chain of being:
    a. held that people and animals were interlinked in importance and equal in their mutual interdependence
    b. held that all human cultures were interlinked and dependent on each other for the health, prosperity, and survival of all
    c. ranked all creatures from inferior to superior, with the wise, innocent, and childlike indigenous peoples at the top of the hierarchy
    * d. ranked all creatures from inferior to superior, with white, "civilized" Western Europeans at the top
    e. none of the above

3. The responses of indigenous peoples to Western colonization included:
    a. adaptation
    b. extinction
    c. cultural disintegration
    d. feelings of security
    e. all of the above
    * f. all of the above except _____ (d)

4. Native systems that were undermined by colonial expansion included systems of:
    a. kinship
    b. subsistence and economy
    c. meaning
    d. health care
    * e. all of the above

5. Disasters of culture as the result of Western colonization occurred in:
    a. Siberia and most of Asia
    b. North and South America
    c. Australia and Tasmania
    d. India and Africa
    e. all of the above except _____
    * f. all of the above

6. From the point of view of the native peoples, the expansion of Europe was:
   a. a tremendous stroke of good fortune
   b. a relatively neutral event
   c. an opportunity to participate in and benefit from the Industrial Revolution and advanced European technologies
   * d. a cataclysmic disaster
   e. all of the above
   f. _____ and _____

7. A colony is:
   * a. a group of people that is under the political hegemony of an alien ruler
   b. a group of people ruled by a local king
   c. a city-state
   d. a subculture living within a larger culture
   e. none of the above

8. Before colonialism, most colonized peoples, generally speaking, had lived in:
   a. perfect peace and tranquility
   b. static and unchanging cultures
   * c. a state of balance with nature
   d. constant warfare and violence
   e. none of the above
   f. _____ and _____

9. Colonizers successfully changed the colonized from subsistence agriculture to wage labor with:
   a. rewards and beneficial incentives
   b. persuasion and education
   c. mutual trust and affection
   d. a high value on self-reliance and independence
   * e. taxes that had to be paid in cash
   f. all of the above

10. Decisions made by colonial powers were always made on the basis of:
    a. the needs of the colonized
    b. the ecological balance
    c. what worked best for both colonizer and colonized
    * d. the needs of the colonizers
    e. none of the above

11. Colonizing governors and missionaries tended to see themselves as:
    a. bearers of misery and despair
    b. robbers and exploiters
    * c. bearers of civilization and the one true religion
    d. scientists and anthropologists doing ethnographic investigations
    e. agents of cultural disintegration and destruction

12. The colonizers who most often had the interests of the indigenous peoples at heart were:
    a. traders
    b. overseers
    c. colonial governors
    d. heads of joint-stock companies
    * e. missionaries
    f. none of the above

13. The impact of colonialism on most of the world's societies occurred between:
    a. 1300-1700
    b. 1700-1800
    * c. 1500-1960
    d. 1800-1990

14. The extinction of the Tasmanians was the result of:
    a. cultural misunderstandings and disease
    b. the brutality of the bush rangers and other settlers
    c. eight thousand years of successful evolution
    d. the Western notion that indigenous peoples were better than whites
    e. all of the above
    * f. ____ and ____ (a and b)

15. The Spanish conquest of the Aztecs succeeded in part because of:
    a. prevailing Aztec mythology
    b. the hatred of the Aztecs by many neighboring tribes
    c. the low level of Aztec cultural development
    d. cultural miscommunication
    e. all of the above
    * f. all of the above except ____ (c)

16. The Yaqui Indians of northern Mexico:
    * a. underwent and ultimately adapted to four complete changes of culture and social space as a result of the Spanish Conquest
    b. were never conquered and subjugated by anyone
    c. ceased to exist as a cultural group as a result of the conquest
    d. became extinct as a people from disease and enslavement
    e. none of the above

17. The most common pattern of the response of indigenous peoples to Western colonial expansion was:
    a. extinction
    b. cultural disintegration and collapse
    c. complete assimilation into the dominant group
    * d. resistance and adaptation
    e. none of the above

18. When traditional explanations and meanings no longer work for current events:
    a. people search for meaning in new religion
    b. people try to relieve the stress by turning to cults
    c. cultural dissonance results
    d. action chains become tenuous
  * e. all of the above
    f. all of the above except ____

19. Millenarian cults are:
    a. social inventions
    b. likely to occur when the culture in people's heads is out-of-phase with the culture in the environment
    c. distinguished by anthropologists from other types of cults
    d. not successful in resolving cultural dissonance
    e. all of the above
  * f. all of the above except ____ (d)

20. Myth is an important element of human life in all situations. It takes on additional importance:
    a. when no practical solution to a given problem exists
    b. when reality is so painful that denying it brings comfort
    c. when people are experiencing extreme cultural dissonance
    d. when people are too intellectually backward to develop scientific explanations
    e. all of the above
  * e. all of the above except ____ (d)

21. The Native American ghost dance:
    a. was a misleading and irrational invention by a fake prophet
    b. occurred at the height of frustration among Native Americans, as they were being settled onto reservations
    c. spread from the Paiute of Nevada to many Native American tribes
    d. was an attempt to solve on a supernatural plane the problems that seemed insoluble in the mundane world
    e. all of the above
  * f. all of the above except ____ (a)

22. The cargo cults of Melanesia:
    a. usually postulated that the ancestors would return and a better day would dawn
    b. were based on the Melanesians' observations that Europeans did not work directly to produce their food, but rather imported it as cargo on boats and planes
    c. prophesied a day when the Melanesians would be on top of the social ranking system
    d. reflected the insecurity and uncertainty of the Melanesians about their future, and their awareness of their lack of control over their own destiny
  * e. all of the above

138

23. The term cultural flight refers to:
    a. members of a given culture who physically run away from contact with other cultures
  * b. changing cultural definitions so that unacceptable situations seem acceptable
    c. metaphysical journeys by shamans and other religious practitioners
    d. none of the above

24. The term Third World:
    a. originally meant the nations that would not join the Cold War by siding with either the capitalist First World or the communist Second World
    b. came during the 1950s to mean the underdeveloped nations of the Earth
    c. includes over one hundred states and about three-fourths of the world's population
    d. consists mainly of countries that were colonized by European powers to produce raw materials for the markets of Europe and, later, Anglo-America
  * e. all of the above
    f. all of the above except _____

25. The interlinking of Third World countries into the global market economy has led to:
    a. a widening of the economic gap between rich and poor countries
    b. a discrepancy in per capita income between rich and poor countries of more than fourteen to one
    c. an increase in agricultural productivity in Third World countries
    d. an increase in hunger and malnutrition in Third World countries
  * e. all of the above
    f. all of the above except _____

26. The Green Revolution in the Third World:
    a. created an additional need for fertilizers, irrigation, and labor practices that require large amounts of capital
    b. drove many individual peasant farmers off the land and into the cities
    c. resulted in the few farmers who were successful at agribusiness hiring some of the formerly independent farmers as wage laborers
    d. switched the householding form of subsistence formerly dominant in Third World countries over to a market economy based on wage labor
  * e. all of the above
    f. all of the above except _____

27. The current utilization of the Third World not just for resources and labor but also as a market for First World goods is known as:
    a. the global market economy
  * b. neo-colonialism
    c. colonialist expansion
    d. mercantilism
    e. none of the above

28. Major problems faced by the postmodern world include:
    a. the fact that inventions in social organization have not kept up with advances in technology
    b. too much reliance on manufacturing and production of goods
    c. millions of people who are either redundant to or in the way of the social and economic systems in which they live
    d. the desire for maintenance of the status quo by many of those currently holding power in the global market economy
    e. all of the above
  * f. all of the above except _____ (b)

29. Planet-wide culture:
    a. is found in institutions that exist in many different parts of the planet, like large corporations and airports
    b. exhibits some regional variations
    c. results from the interdependencies of institutions in all parts of the earth
    d. is indicated in the term global village
  * e. all of the above

30. Small cultural groups whose members do not live in geographical proximity:
    a. have dramatically increased in number due to modern means of communication
    b. allow many individuals in the postmodern world to participate in many different cultures in one lifetime
    c. insure that the world will remain immensely rich in cultures
    d. allow the formation of cultures based on common personal interests
  * e. all of the above
    f. all of the above except _____

31. Some of the attributes of the emerging global society pointed to by Bohannan as needing investigation through anthropological thinking and research include:
    a. the emergence of "the person" and new kinds of family
    b. the shift from an industrial to a service economy occurring in places like the U.S.
    c. constant culture change
    d. the emergence of a social network based on the principle of hierarchy
    e. all of the above
  * f. all of the above except _____ (d)

32. A SPIN is *not*:
    a. a segmented, polycephalous, idea-based network
  * b. a form of bureaucratic hierarchy
    c. a new kind of social organization
    d. a generalized network of equals drawn together by the power of shared interests and convictions
    e. all of the above

33. New mythologies whose villain is "the system":
   * a. are a feature of the emerging global society
   b. express the continuity of culture so characteristic of the postmodern world
   c. characterize the cargo cults of the Melanesians
   d. are typical of millenarian cults in general
   e. all of the above

Essay

1. What were the two concepts that, according to Bohannan, blinded the Europeans in their efforts to relate to the indigenous peoples of the colonial world? Describe these concepts and explain their effects on the behavior of the colonizers.

2. Briefly describe the role of missionaries in the colonization of indigenous peoples.

3. Describe the European expansion during the colonial period from the point of view of both the colonizers and the colonized.

4. How long had the Tasmanians been living on their island before first contact with whites? What happened to them? Why? Could their fate have been avoided? If so, how?

5. Was the Spanish conquest of Mexico inevitable? Upon what did its success depend? What was its ultimate result?

6. What do you think might have happened if Cortes had not reached the coast of Mexico in the Year of the Reed, but instead had arrived in a mythologically neutral year? What ultimate effect, if any, might this have had on European colonial expansion into South and Central America?

7. What happened to indigenous cultures as the result of colonial expansion? What was the most typical response of such cultures?

8. What can we learn from the Yaqui about human cultural adaptability?

9. Why is the adjustment to new culture more difficult under situations of conquest or colonialism?

10. What is cultural dissonance? How did some peoples cope with the cultural dissonance introduced by colonialism? What does that have to do with cultural flight?

11. What did the ghost dance originated by the Paiute and the cargo cults of the Melanesians have in common? What purposes did they serve, and why did they come into being when they did?

12. Using specific examples, describe the relationship between millenarian cults and cultural flight.

13. What are the origins of the term Third World? What does it mean today?

14. How was the Third World formed? Why is it "underdeveloped"? In relation to what is it "underdeveloped"? Who sets the standard for "development" and what does that suggest about the future of Third World nations?

15. Explain this paradox: at the same time that agricultural production in the Third World has been increasing dramatically as the result of the Green Revolution, hunger and malnutrition have also dramatically increased.

16. What is neo-colonialism and what are the implications of that term?

17. Why does Bohannan say that we live in a two-story cultural world? What realities of postmodern life is he trying to illustrate with that metaphor?

18. How do today's notions of "human rights" and the "person as process" differ from the view of earlier industrial periods in which "individuals" were parts of society in much the same way that cogs and wheels were parts of machines? What are the sociocultural implications for individuals today?

19. What is a SPIN? Why are SPINs important in the postmodern world? What change in cultural style and values does their emergence reflect?

20. Name and discuss at least three of the attributes of the emerging global society Bohannan points to at the end of Chapter 14.

Anthropology in a Global Society

15

What students should get out of the chapter . . .

If it is a human characteristic to change whatever is uncomfortable or unrewarding, then we can learn to build culture more efficiently and can improve the human lot. Practicing anthropology is expanding into problems of medicine, law, government, business. Visionary anthropology is expanding into the study of clearer visions of the present social and cultural condition and of possible futures.

Films and Videos

Maragoli. 58 min. color. 1978. University of California Extension Media Center. Perceptive document on the social and economic problems of village life in the Third World, using the Maragoli region of western Kenya as a case study. The people of Maragoli tell their side of the "development" story: their perception of their needs and aspirations, the reasons they must have as many children as they do, their feelings about the destruction of their traditional lifeways, and their fears for the future of their families. An "insider's view" of the interlocking problems of high birthrates, food shortages, land scarcity, unequal access to education, unemployment, and migration.

Papua New Guinea: Anthropology on Trial. 57 min. color. 1983. Indiana University Audio-Visual Center. Addresses the practice of remote tribes and exotic islanders being made known to the world through the interpretation of anthropologists. Reports the objections of some of these people who have been the subject of studies. Looks at anthropology from the other side.

The Spirit of Ethnography. 18 min. black and white. 1974. Penn State Audio-Visual Services. A satire on the basic processes of data gathering in cultural anthropology. Chronicles the field research of a fictitious ethnographer embarking on his first field experience. Humorous view of anthropologists making fun of themselves and some of the classic ethnographic films.

Chapter 15

Test Items

True/False

1. The gravest global problems are social and cultural.   **T**

2. Technology is always invented and utilized in ways that reflect social and cultural values.   **T**

3. According to Bohannan, the gravest danger in capitalist countries is that they will interpret the overthrow of the communist system in the USSR as meaning that they were right all along.   **T**

4. Social science, which underlies social policy, has been able to develop more rapidly than physical science, which underlies technology.   **F**

5. The technological and scientific knowledge needed to solve the global problems of environmental pollution and global hunger is unavailable at the present time.   **F**

6. According to Bohannan, one of the most needed studies in the social sciences is a comprehensive survey of the social traps that humans have fallen into in the past and present, so that we can work to avoid them in the future.   **T**

7. Bohannan believes that computer simulations may soon be used to study the potential long-range impact of social and cultural changes or trends.   **T**

8. Possible ways to solve the drug problem in the U.S. include making possession of even a small amount of drugs a capital offense, and legalizing drugs and taxing their sale to fund nationwide free treatment centers for addicts.   **T**

9. Visionary anthropology tries to make a difference by working with the culture already at hand to solve immediate social problems.   **F**

10. Contemporary anthropologists work only in academic settings.   **F**

11. The ideas of scientific medicine are often at odds with the patients' own perceptions of the causes and progress of their diseases and ailments.   **T**

12. Positive aspects of American medicine include its renowned compassionate, caring and empathetic approach to healing.   **F**

13. Medical anthropologists seek to understand the healing systems of other cultures by uncovering the deep cultural beliefs that provide the rationale for their cures.   **T**

14. In Yoruba belief, simple illnesses are said to result from an imbalance in the body of substances that normally would contribute to health.   **T**

15. In Western belief, most illnesses are seen as invasions of the body.   **T**

16. A logical extension of Western belief about disease is that it is a normal part of life that is best kept under control by moral, balanced living.   **F**

17. Scientific medicine usually integrates the spiritual dimensions of healing with its technological cures.   **F**

18. Common assumptions of healing systems from other cultures are that the body is a reflection of the natural energies flowing within it and that illness is caused by blockages of energy paths.   **T**

19. In business, the "science of management" depends heavily on anthropological theory applied to the corporation.   T

20. Anthropologists specializing in business often conduct economic studies of corporate culture.   F

21. Within corporations, anthropologists can improve communication and point out and help eliminate social traps.   T

22. Unfortunately, anthropologists have been of little help to businesses trying to conduct business in other cultures.   F

23. According to Bohannan, we are presently living on the cusp of a culture crest.   T

24. Visionary anthropologists are actively engaged in creating social policy for a successful future.   T

25. In all likelihood, bureaucracies will be more useful and relevant to the emerging global society than ever before.   F

26. Prediction in social science is rendered relatively simple by the fact that contexts can easily be kept constant.   F

27. Changing the scale of social groups can demonstrate that previously adequate social systems and institutions are no longer sufficient and change must occur.   T

28. Prediction in social science is the same as foretelling the future.   F

29. Every time social scientists change focus from one culture to another, they must re-examine all their basic assumptions.   T

30. One reason that we cannot predict the future is that the adaptive capacity of choice-making has been built into human beings in the course of evolution.   T

31. Ethnographic futures research is based on the premise that anthropologists can determine what people think is going to happen in the future.   T

32. According to Bohannan, a social trap contained in futures research is that people may create new ideology to counteract the information discovered by the researcher.   T

33. Policy science is recognized for its precision.   F

34. Ideally, policy science will create early warning systems for social traps.   T

35. The boundary between visionary anthropology and science fiction is clear.   F

36. The fact that genetic changes occurring in small, isolated populations can spread rapidly implies that, if human beings populate space stations or other planets, the biological evolution of humans could take entirely new forms.   T

Multiple Choice

1. Bohannan stresses that the gravest global problems are:
    a. technological
    b. environmental
    c. physical
  * d. social and cultural
    e. all of the above
    f. all of the above except _____

146

2. Technology is always invented and utilized:
    a. in the most enlightened ways possible
    b. in culturally neutral ways
 * c. in ways that reflect social and cultural values
    d. in isolated contexts
    e. none of the above

3. Environmental catastrophes, homelessness, the deteriorating educational system, the AIDS epidemic, and the difficulties that beset Eastern Europe, are all:
    a. technological problems
    b. examples of how impossible it is to live together successfully in groups
 * c. social problems
    d. environmental problems
    e. all of the above

4. According to Bohannan, politicization of social science may sometimes be:
    a. necessary for the development of future policy
    b. inevitable
 * c. a social trap
    d. impossible
    e. a futuristic scenario

5. Social scientists cannot:
    a. use computer simulations to help them test theories and predictions
    b. predict the future
    c. hold context constant in their social experiments
    d. understand the belief and value systems underlying many of the policy decisions being made
    e. do any of the above
 * f. _____ and _____ (b and c)

6. Solution of contemporary global problems is currently impeded by:
    a. poor scientific understanding of the nature of these problems
    b. lack of the technological means of solving them
 * c. lack of information about the social, behavioral, and economic consequences of the various possible solutions
    d. all of the above

7. Before the middle 1950s, anthropologists who tried to make a difference in the real world dealt almost exclusively with:
    a. envisioning and implementing new social policies
    b. trying to understand the emerging global society
    c. easing the workings of contemporary American society
 * d. repairing injustices to colonized peoples
    e. all of the above

8. The safest and most promising way to test potential solutions to social problems is to:
    a. implement them into social policy through law and see what happens
    b. conduct surveys and polls on what people think would happen
  * c. use computer simulations to project the most likely results
    d. publish possible solutions so that people would be exposed to—and therefore more likely to accept—them
    e. none of the above

9. Visionary anthropology tries to make a difference by:
    a. recognizing and analyzing emerging cultural and social developments
    b. helping to recontext cultural ways from other places and times
    c. dreaming up new cultural and social tools that have never existed
    d. working primarily with the culture already at hand to solve problems with a deadline
    e. all of the above
  * f. all of the above except ____ (d)

10. Today, anthropologists can be found at work in:
    a. medicine
    b. businesses and corporations
    c. the World Bank
    d. planning commissions
  * e. all of the above
    f. all of the above except ____

11. The Tiv husband whose wife was stung by the scorpion:
    a. revealed his ignorance and the primitive level of his tribal medicine by making more than one incision on her skin
    b. was following Tiv theory that the poison travels up through veins and tendons, then falls into the stomach by trying to short stop the poison
    c. failed to help his wife at all with so many extra incisions
    d. in following beliefs that his wife shared, helped to make her calmer, to lessen her fear and pain
    e. all of the above except ____
  * f. ____ and ____ (b and d)

12. Problems inherent in modern medicine include:
    a. differences in perception on the part of patients and doctors about causes, progress, and meaning of the ailment
    b. the fact that it gets more and more expensive as it becomes more technologically developed
    c. differential access to health care between wealthy and poor
    d. reliance on technology as a dehumanizing force
  * e. all of the above
    f. all of the above except ____

13. Medical anthropologists:
    a. talk to curers in many cultures to uncover the deep cultural beliefs that provide the rationale for their cures
    b. try to assist traditional healers in discussing their knowledge with each other and with healers from other cultures, including Western physicians
    c. study the relationships between disease and nutrition, population growth rates, reproduction and birth control, epidemics such as AIDS, and historical plagues
  * d. all of the above
    f. all of the above except _____

14. The Yoruba think some diseases are caused by:
    a. confusion of colors
    b. excess of certain substances in the body
    c. handling dirty money
    d. revealing things that are supposed to be hidden
    e. all of the above
  * f. all of the above except _____(c)

15. Ancient medical traditions from East Asia, India, and the Greek-Arabic world:
    a. reveal the dissimilarity in different cultural approaches to healing and health
    b. assume that the body is a reflection of the natural energies flowing within it
    c. assume that illness is caused by blockages in the energy paths
    d. call on people to eat sensibly, and to live temperately and morally
    e. all of the above
  * f. all of the above except _____ (a)

16. Contributions that anthropology can make to business include:
    a. providing a theoretical framework for business policies
    b. ethnographies of corporate cultures
    c. insights into relationships in the workplace and with customers
    d. assistance with communication skills within companies and between cultures
  * e. all of the above
    f. all of the above except _____

17. Examples of the rapid culture change currently sweeping the globe include:
  * a. interlinkings of individuals in all parts of the globe through technological systems of communication
    b. mercantilism and colonialism
    c. the Industrial Revolution
    d. the end of the last ice age
    e. the transition from hunting and gathering to agriculture

149

18. Change of scale in human society:
    a. is usually of little relevance when the social forms that preceded the change of scale have been functioning smoothly for a long time
    * b. can ensure that previously adequate social forms and institutions are no longer sufficient and new forms must be implemented
    c. has nothing to do with human cycles and trajectories
    d. is based on Bohannan's theory of prediction and chaos
    e. all of the above
    f. _____ and _____

19. Prediction in social science:
    a. causes chaos
    b. requires a re-examination of all basic assumptions every time the social scientist changes focus from one culture to another
    c. is possible and useful when context is relatively constant
    d. is the same as foretelling the future
    e. all of the above
    * f. _____ and _____ (b and c)

20. Reasons why social scientists cannot accurately predict the future include:
    a. the fact that social context cannot be held constant
    b. the adaptive human capacity to make individual choices that differ from the norm
    c. kinship theory and theories of social organization
    d. cycles and trajectories
    e. all of the above
    * f. _____ and _____ (a and b)

21. Ethnographic futures research:
    a. involves trying to determine what people think is going to happen
    b. is a social scientific form of fortunetelling
    c. can sometimes point out the places where change is most likely to occur, and pinpoint potential social traps
    d. all of the above
    * e. _____ and _____ (a and c)

22. Policy science:
    a. is recognized for its precision
    b. ideally will create early warning systems for social traps
    c. uses only social science to present choices to policy makers
    d. uses computer simulation to show the possible results of introducing different variables into the current system
    e. all of the above
    * f. _____ and _____ (b and d)

23. The fuzziness of the boundary between visionary anthropology and science fiction is revealed in:
   a. the fact that space exploration and settlement were in the realm of science fiction only a few decades ago and now exist in reality
   b. the fact that the biological evolution of humans could take entirely new forms
   c. the cross-cultural nature of current space explorations and cooperative ventures
   d. the reality that new forms of culture and government will have to be created
   e. the impact of space travel and space settlement of life on Planet Earth
   * f. all of the above

Essay

1. Why does Bohannan stress that the gravest global problems are social and cultural, not technological? What does this imply for their possible solution?

2. Is technology culturally neutral? In other words, is technology simply a set of tools, or is it always invented and utilized in ways that reflect social and cultural values? Discuss, using specific examples.

3. As Bohannan mentions in Chapter 15, when Senator Patrick Moynihan was asked in a television interview why we could put people on the moon but could not solve our social problems, he answered, "You see, there wasn't anybody who didn't want to go to the moon." What did he mean, and what does his answer have to do with Bohannan's statement that the politicization of social science is a social trap?

4. What, according to Bohannan, is the primary difference between research in the physical and social sciences?

5. In Chapter 15, Bohannan states, "What both social scientists and statesmen need is an early warning system of changes in the context of achieving goals and struggling against chaos." Explain this statement. What is the "context" he speaks of? Why do social scientists and statesmen need to be warned about changes in this context? How might such a warning system be developed, and what good would it do?

6. What role does Bohannan project for computer simulations in policy science? Why?

7. Do you agree that we "desperately need a good survey of social traps"? What good would such a survey do us?

8. What would be the advantage of testing new social policies by computer simulation before they are tried out in actual practice?

9. In Chapter 15, Bohannan presents two possible solutions to the drug problem in the U.S.: 1) making the use of drugs a capital offense and firmly carrying that out; and 2) legalizing drugs, taxing them, and using the tax money to fund nationwide free treatment programs for addicts.

   Keeping in mind Bohannan's string-of-beads analogy (changing one part of a culture affects all the rest), compare and contrast these two solutions in terms of the changes in beliefs and values each would require and their likely long-term effects. Conclude either by strongly recommending one of these two solutions, or by making a strong case for a solution of your own.

10. Why are anthropologists often called on to serve as cultural brokers in business? medicine? education? What are some of the roles they play in these areas, and of what value are their services?

11. It is an anthropological premise that people's ideas about the way the body works and the way medicine works in the body are usually closely tied up with their views of the cosmos and how it works.

   a. Cite two examples from other cultures, and explain the connections in some detail.

   b. Consider American culture. How does the American medical system seem to think the body works/medicine works in the body, and are those notions connected to our cultural views of the cosmos and how it works? Discuss in detail.

12. What are some of the benefits of the American medical system? Some of the drawbacks? How might some of these drawbacks be altered if our medical system were to seek to incorporate more elements from other cultures? What effect would such elements have on that system?

13. Compare and contrast Yoruba and American ideas about health and illness. What can you conclude?

14. What do the ancient medical traditions of East Asia, India, and the Greek-Arabic world have in common? How do the basic premises of our own medical system differ from the premises of these three traditions? To what do you attribute this difference?

15. What roles do anthropologists play in today's business world?

16. What is visionary anthropology? Where is the boundary between it and science fiction?

17. Cite and discuss at least three examples of the effects of changes of scale on social groups and the social institutions they create.

18. What is ethnographic futures research?

19. Identify and discuss at least three potential effects of space settlement on the human cultures that remain on earth.

20. Do you think that our human capacity to use culture against ourselves will ultimately destroy us? Why or why not?

1. Discuss action chains, event chains, cycles, and trajectories. Why are these concepts useful for the understanding of cultural behavior? What do they have to do with policy considerations?

2. Explain the relationship between action chains and social traps, using specific examples.

3. Describe an action chain that is cyclical, and one that is a trajectory. What can you say about the worldviews underlying each type?

4. Why did the Europeans expand? How did native peoples react?

5. How is new culture usually created and spread? Why is the adjustment to new culture more difficult under situations of conquest or colonialism? What did some colonized people do to deal with that difficulty?

6. Discuss the differences and relationships between mercantilism, capitalism, colonialism, neo-colonialism, and the global market economy.

7. Why does the capitalist system produce poverty in the Third World and at home? What is the solution to this social trap? Why hasn't this trap been eliminated to date?

8. a. In Chapter 15, Bohannan suggests that possible solutions to social problems can be tested by computer simulation. Pick any three of the following social problems, and suggest two possible solutions to each that could be so tested:

drug use in the U.S.	the situation of the Iraqi Kurds
poverty and homelessness	ethnic unrest in the USSR
environmental pollution and destruction	global overpopulation
the danger of nuclear war	the AIDS epidemic
the burgeoning costs of medical care	hunger and malnutrition
the Arab-Israeli conflict and the problem of the Palestinians	the hole in the ozone layer

   b. What social changes would your solutions require? Do you think they would be possible to accomplish, or would the social upheaval they cause be too great, so that the solution would be worse than the problem?

9. Consider yourself both an anthropologist engaged in ethnographic futures research and an informant for that researcher. As the informant, write three pages about what you think is going to happen in the world in the next fifty years. Then review your data to find out:

   a. What are the cultural and historical roots of your projections?

   b. What computer simulations you might wish to run, and what you might learn from them?

   c. What policy recommendations you might wish to make?

1. What does the religion of the Aranda have to do with the fact that they are hunter-gatherers? What does Christianity in its modern form have to do with the fact that we have until recently been an industrial society? What does the religion of the Huichol have to do with the fact that they once hunted and gathered, but now are agriculturalists? What can you conclude about the relationship of religion to subsistence method?

2. Discuss the transformation of earlier economic forms by the advent of capitalism.

3. How do you think the people of the twenty-second century on Planet Earth will answer the eternal questions?

4. What is the role of kinship in culture and what resulted from the undermining of native kinship systems by governors and missionaries during the colonial period?

5. Pick a society that is cycle-oriented and one that is trajectory-oriented. Compare and contrast their subsistence methods, worldviews, values, and responses to rapid change.

6. What is a millenarian cult? How are millenarian cults different from the other types of cults discussed in Chapter 12?

7. Discuss the relationship between cults and cultural stress, using specific examples.

8. According to Bohannan, "the fact that inventions in social organization have not kept up with advances in technology has created problems." What are some of these problems? What social inventions are needed to solve them?

9. Why is culture like a string of beads? What are the implications of that metaphor for small cultures that come into contact with large ones? for culture change? for the global society? for the scientific study of culture?

10. If a major environmental disaster should strike the U.S. during your presidency, how might you as leader of the nation use your anthropological knowledge to stave off complete social disintegration? (Assume functional communications systems in your answer.)

11. What was the effect of the metaphor of the great chain of being in its time? How did it get tied in to the idea of evolution? What did it have to do with mercantilism and colonialism? And what is its legacy to our time?

12. Describe and discuss some of the questions that marked anthropology's origins. Compare them to some of the new questions that mark its concerns today and for the future.

13. Using specific societies from your readings as examples, explain the differences between hunter-gatherer, horticultural, agricultural, industrial, and postindustrial societies (*choose any three of these*) in terms of at least *four* of the following categories:

> social values, norms, worldview, religion
> social and political organization
> economic organization and division of labor
> gender relations
> population size and density
> relationship to the environment
> _____ (a category of your choosing)

14. a. How would you like the humans on the earth to be living in the twenty-second century? Describe earth society as you would like to see it become. Utilize the categories listed in Question #13 to help you organize your thoughts and *be specific. Avoid platitudes.*

    b. Now use your anthropological insight to make very specific policy recommendations that we might begin to implement now to get us to your vision by the year 2100.

15. Who is the alien? What does it mean to be human?

16. Create a native culture describing its systems and beliefs about kinship, sex, gender, power, communication and religion. Pretend you are an anthropological fieldworker studying this culture. Describe your feelings about your surroundings and the people. What insights about your own culture must you address and understand in order to understand and appreciate the native culture you are studying?

Appendix I

The following is an up-to-date list of distribution centers for the films annotated in this guide. Call for copies of their film and video rental and sales catalogs. Most contain fairly detailed subject indexes as well as useful descriptions similar to the ones provided for the selected films in this guide. Formats and prices vary.

Audience Planners
5107 Douglas Fir Road
Calabasas, California 91302
818/884-3100

Brigham Young University
Audio Visual Services/Scheduling
Fletcher Building
Provo, Utah 84602
801/378-2713

Direct Cinema Limited
P.O. Box 69799
Los Angeles, California 90069
213/652-8000

Documentary Educational Resources
101 Morse Street
Watertown, Massachusetts 02172
617/926-0491

El Nil Research
1147 Beverwill Drive
Los Angeles, California 90035
213/553-5645

Films Incorporated Video
5547 North Ravenswood Avenue
Chicago, Illinois 60640-1199
800/323-4222; in Illinois call 312/878-2600

Indiana University Audio-Visual Center
Bloomington, Indiana 47405-5901
800/552-8620; in Indiana call 812/855-2103

The Museum of Modern Art
Film Department
11 West 53d Street
New York, New York 10019-5498
212/708-9400

Penn State Audio-Visual Services
University Division of Media and Learning Resources
Special Services Building
The Pennsylvania State University
University Park, Pennsylvania 16802
800/826-0132

University of California Extension Media Center
2176 Shattuck Avenue
Berkeley, California 94704
510/642-0460

University of Illinois Film and Video Center
1325 South Oak Street
Champaign, Illinois 61820
217/333-1360

University of Minnesota
University Film and Video
Continuing Education and Extension
1313 Fifth Street, S.E.
Suite 108
Minneapolis, Minnesota 55414
800/847-8251; in Minnesota call 612/627-4270

University of Wisconsin
Center for South Asian Studies
1236 Van Hise Hall
1220 Linden Drive
Madison, Wisconsin 53706
608/262-3209

Reference:

Consult these regularly-updated sources in your library for help in locating a film:

The Educational Film and Video Locator
The Film and Video Finder

Appendix II

Case Studies available from Waveland Press, Inc.

Aguilera, *Santa Eulalia's People*
Alkire, *Lamotrek Atoll and Inter-island Socioeconomic Ties*
Alland, *When the Spider Danced: Notes from an African Village*
Anderson, *First Fieldwork*
Arensberg, *The Irish Countryman: An Anthropological Study*
Aschenbrenner, *Lifelines: Black Families in Chicago*
Balikci, *The Netsilik Eskimo*
Barrett, *Benabarre: The Modernization of a Spanish Village*
Barth, *Nomads of South Persia*
Bascom, *The Yoruba of Southwestern Nigeria*
Basso, *The Cibecue Apache*
Basso, *The Kalapalo Indians of Central Brazil*
Bastien, *Mountain of the Condor*
Bauman, *Let Your Words Be Few*
Beidelman, *The Kaguru: A Matrilineal People of East Africa*
Biesanz et al., *The Costa Ricans*
Blok, *The Mafia of a Sicilian Village, 1860-1960*
Bohannan, *Justice and Judgment among the Tiv*
Bowes, *Kibbutz Goshen: An Israeli Commune*
Brana-Shute, *On the Corner*
Brandt, *A Korean Village: Between Farm and Sea*
Cassell, *A Group Called Women*
Chiñas, *La Zandunga*
Cohen, *The Kanuri of Borno*
Cooper, *The Wood-carvers of Hong Kong*
Crumrine, *The Mayo Indians of Sonora*
Davidson, *Chicano Prisoners: The Key to San Quentin*
Deng, *The Dinka of the Sudan*
de Rios, *Visionary Vine*
Downs, *The Navajo*
Dozier, *The Pueblo Indians of North America*
Dumont, *The Headman and I*
Dunn-Dunn, *The Peasants of Central Russia*
Dwyer, *Moroccan Dialogues: Anthropology in Question*
Ekvall, *Fields on the Hoof*
Fakhouri, *Kafr el-Elow, 2/e*
Faron, *The Mapuche Indians of Chile*
Fernea, *A Street in Marrakech*
Fernea-Fernea, *Nubian Ethnographies*
Fortune, *Sorcerers of Dobu*
Foster, *Tzintzuntzan: Mexican Peasants in a Changing World*
Frankenberg, *Village on the Border*
Fraser, *Fishermen of South Thailand: The Malay Villagers*
Freeman, *Scarcity and Opportunity in an Indian Village*
Gamst, *The Qemant: A Pagan-Hebraic Peasantry of Ethiopia*
Garbarino, *Big Cypress: A Changing Seminole Community*
Geertz, *The Javanese Family*
Gmelch, *The Irish Tinkers, 2/e*
Gmelch, *Nan: The Life of an Irish Travelling Woman*
Gold, *St. Pascal*
Halpern-Halpern, *A Serbian Village in Historical Perspective*
Hanson, *Rapan Lifeways*
Harris, *Casting Out Anger: Religion among the Taita of Kenya*
Hayano, *Road Through the Rain Forest*
Hickerson, *The Chippewa and Their Neighbors*
Hicks, *Appalachian Valley*
Hicks, *Tetum Ghosts and Kin*
Holmberg, *Nomads of the Long Bow*
Howell, *Hard Living on Clay Street*
Isbell, *To Defend Ourselves*

Islam, *A Bangladesh Village: Political Conflict and Cohesion*
Jablow, *Gassire's Lute: A West African Epic*
Jacobs, *Fun City*
Jacobson, *Itinerant Townsmen*
Jones-Jones, *The Himalayan Woman*
Kearney, *The Winds of Ixtepeji*
Kertzer, *Comrades and Christians*
Kiefer, *The Tausug*
Klass, *East Indians in Trinidad*
Klima, *The Barabaig: East African Cattle-herders*
Kolenda, *Caste in Contemporary India*
LaFlamme, *Green Turtle Cay: An Island in the Bahamas*
Lawrence, *Road Belong Cargo*
Lessa, *Ulithi: A Micronesian Design for Living*
Loewen, *The Mississippi Chinese, 2/e*
Macfarlane, *Witchcraft in Tudor and Stuart England*
Mahmood, *Frisian and Free*
Malinowski, *Argonauts of the Western Pacific*
McFee, *Modern Blackfeet: Montanans on a Reservation*
Messenger, *Inis Beag: Isle of Ireland*
Miller, *Old Villages and New Towns: Industrialization of Mexico*
Mitchell, *The Bamboo Fire: An Anthropologist in New Guinea, 2/e*
Nash, *In the Eyes of the Ancestors*
Norbeck, *Changing Japan, 2/e*
Ohnuki-Tierney, *The Ainu of the Northwest Coast of Southern Sakhalin*
Partridge, *The Hippie Ghetto*
Pelto, *The Snowmobile Revolution*
Preston, *Cult of the Goddess*
Quintana-Floyd, *¡Qué Gitano!: Gypsies of Southern Spain*
Read, *Children of Their Fathers: Growing Up among the Ngoni*
Reck, *In the Shadow of Tlaloc: Life in a Mexican Village*
Redfield-Villa Rojas, *Chan Kom: A Maya Village*
Richardson, *San Pedro, Colombia*
Ritzenthaler-Ritzenthaler, *The Woodland Indians of the Western Great Lakes*
Rohner-Bettauer, *The Kwakiutl: Indians of British Columbia*
Rosenfeld, *"Shut Those Thick Lips!"*
Rosman-Rubel, *Feasting with Mine Enemy*
Salzmann-Scheufler, *Komárov: A Czech Farming Village*
Schaffer-Cooper, *Mandinko*
Sexton, *Son of Tecún Umán*
Skinner, *The Mossi of Burkina Faso*
Spindler-Spindler, *Dreamers with Power: The Menominee*
Sutherland, *Gypsies: The Hidden Americans*
Sutlive, *The Iban of Sarawak: Chronicle of a Vanishing World*
van Beek, *The Kapsiki of the Mandara Hills*
Vigil, *From Indians to Chicanos*
Wagley, *Welcome of Tears: The Tapirapé Indians of Central Brazil*
Ward, *Nest in the Wind*
Ward, *Them Children: A Study in Language Learning*
Wax et al., *Formal Education in an American Indian Community*
Whiteford, *Two Cities of Latin America*
Whitten, *Black Frontiersmen*
Williams, *Community in a Black Pentecostal Church*
Wilson, *Good Company: A Study of Nyakyusa Age-villages*
Wolcott, *A Kwakiutl Village and School*
Wolcott, *The Man in the Principal's Office: An Ethnography*
Yoors, *Crossing: A Journal of Survival and Resistance in WWII*
Yoors, *The Gypsies*